Other works by Daniel D. Ziegler

NAKED BEFORE GOD: *A Look at Healing, Self-discovery and Spiritual Growth Through Social Nudism*

PAZZI WAN: *A Play in Three Acts*

MW01094957

NAKED BEFORE GOD II

Less-Ons For Truth

by

DANIEL D. ZIEGLER

NAKED BEFORE GOD
Less-Ons for Truth
by
Daniel D. Ziegler

Table of Contents

Acknowledgements

First, I want to thank my dear writer friend, Shirley Swift, for pointing me in the direction of a publisher to finally get the original NAKED BEFORE GOD into print. It was a work-in-progress for twenty years and long overdue.

Next, I want to thank my editor for the hours she spent going over the original NAKED BEFORE GOD checking for errors, and for doing the same with this manuscript, NAKED BEFORE GOD II. You showed up completely unexpectedly for both projects. You are a gift; what a delight working with you.

And, I want to thank those readers who read, some more than once, the e-copy of the original NAKED BEFORE GOD, with all its mistakes, before a hard copy was available. Your interest was my inspiration for putting together this book, NAKED BEFORE GOD II.

Dedication

To our future selves who will look back and be thankful "we finally got it."

Preface to the original
NAKED BEFORE GOD

The events leading to the writing of this book are a demonstration of the Universe's support in living our dreams and fulfilling our missions. When we truly focus on what it is we want to do and are willing to get ourselves out of the way, the Universe steps in to create its reality. From my first visit to a nudist park, I knew that social nudism was a profound, life-changing experience that I wanted to bring to the attention of others. I began by sharing it with my friends, taking them to the park with me whenever I could, writing short pieces on my computer and generally spending a lot of time formulating my ideas pertaining to the appeal and the benefits of the nudist experience. The more I focused on these, the more I realized that perhaps I was on the path leading to my long sought-after mission.

Shortly after my introduction to nudism, I left my salary job as a security guard at General Motors. I had spent fifteen years at a reasonably good-paying job that provided good benefits with which to raise my family, but it left part of me unfulfilled. The job, however, did allow me plenty of opportunity to read, study and write, and it was during this fifteen year period that much of my personal and spiritual philosophy took shape.

In December of 1987, four months after I discovered social nudism, the company offered me a cash buy-out and, unhesitatingly, I accepted. I didn't know what I was going to do next, but I knew I no longer wanted to be doing that. My family was raised, I was now divorced, and I felt it was time for something new. I trusted that the Universe would help me find it.

I began looking for opportunities to work within the nudist community. Though there were a few jobs available, most of these were caretaker or grounds keepers jobs, that although would allow me to work in a nudist setting, they were not jobs that would avail me to do what I felt I was most capable of doing, that is, writing and speaking.

Still, willing to do whatever the Universe required, I applied for a couple of these jobs. One was a care taker's job at Elysium Fields, a nudist facility in California, to which founder/owner Ed Lange responded that I was over qualified. Another was a grounds keeper job at Forest Hills, a small nudist park in Michigan, which at the last minute decided against making immediate changes in its staff. Interestingly enough, not being hired in these positions was not disappointing. Something inside told me that there were better things in store for me, that the Universe had a better plan and all that I had to do was to be patient.

The next six years provided me with some difficult but valuable lessons in being patient and in letting go and surrendering. I bounced around the country, going through the motions of looking for work, getting turned down for jobs that I really didn't want, staying with friends, selling my belongings, caring for an Alzheimer's patient, living with a college student son, working minimum wage jobs and generally living on the edge of uncertainty. And, I was learning to trust the Universe–several times being faced with not knowing where my next meal was coming from, but never once ever missing one.

Throughout this period, my interest in writing and speaking about the self-discovery and spiritual aspects of social nudism intensified. In my travels, I managed to visit a number of nudist parks around the country and each time my conviction about the positive effects of this lifestyle was renewed and strengthened. Also, as I continued talking to people–nudists and non-nudists alike–formulating my ideas, I was becoming more aware that my approach to promoting social nudism was different than that of many other nudists. Rather than directing my energies toward fighting for our rights, which I feel is somewhat of a fear-based approach, I was focusing on informing and educating, a love-based approach. I was not so much interested in promoting a movement as I was in helping individuals discover who they are. I was becoming a teacher, not a soldier–and the movement desperately needed teachers.

Through my continuing interest and efforts, I was eventually invited to give a talk on nudism to a group of hypno-therapists, and I was asked to speak on nudism as a guest on a public access TV talk show. The talk with the therapists made me realize that, 1) I needed a nudist park with which I could work closely to follow up the talks with actual visits, and 2) I had to write a book which would be the basis for my talks. The TV interview turned out extremely well showing me that I had an ability to communicate in a direct yet laid-back manner that was reassuring, even inviting.

The serendipitous events that led to the talk and TV interview clearly indicated that the Universe was supporting my efforts, and I was beginning to feel that I was on a definite and *guided* mission. I didn't want to do anything else. I felt it was still necessary, however, for me to continue working at my present minimum wage job, at least for now. This did not seem to be too much of an inconvenience because the job, again, was providing me with time to read, study and write. In fact, some of the material I was to write, I would be using, almost intact, a year later at my next job.

Through the years, I had read many books on motivation, finding your dreams, overcoming fear, self-discovery, spiritual growth, following intuition and other related topics. I also listened to speakers, bought tapes, went to seminars and learned how others were finding their dreams and fulfilling their missions. These activities continually gave me the encouragement needed to carry on even in the most desperate of times.

A friend had once given me a book that described an exercise in which one writes down what they consider to be their ideal work. I had not done the exercise the first time I read the book, but one day as I was day dreaming, the perfect job came to mind. I again thought of the book and decided to do the exercise. I wrote that the perfect job for me was *"a tour guide at a nudist park"*. The book also stated that one need not be logical or practical since the Universe could support any dream that came from a place of love. I certainly wasn't being logical or practical because I knew of no nudist park large enough to require a tour guide, and I was coming from a place of love, my motivation being the opportunity to change people's lives. I realized too, that if there were such a job, it probably wouldn't pay much, but that was not a concern. How I might be compensated, I would leave up to the Universe.

'A tour guide at a nudist park'–I put it out to the Universe.

In September 1993, 1 once again found myself in a situation requiring change. Fifteen months earlier, with no other place to go, I had temporarily moved in with my brother who was living in a one bedroom apartment. As it turned out, the Universe timed my move perfectly because my brother had just suffered a relapse of a previous health condition and required someone to look after him. I was able to be there with him during that time, but now, fifteen months later, after yet another relapse, we decided that it would be in his best interest if he moved into an adult foster care home. As I felt my move into his apartment was guided by the Universe, now I strongly sensed it was now telling me it was time to move on once again.

I gave my employer a two week notice and the landlord a one month notice. I had no idea what I would be doing next. All I knew was that I had some basic ideas for a book I wanted to write, that I wanted to become a tour guide at a nudist park and that after my last day on the job, I would have two weeks to do whatever I wanted to do before I had to be out of the apartment.

I released it all to the Universe.

After my last day on the job, I decided to drive from Auburn Hills, Michigan, where I had been living, to Oshkosh, Wisconsin to meet some of the people at the Naturist Society with whom I had corresponded discussing some of my ideas on promoting naturism (another term for nudism). I thought this would be a good opportunity to meet them in person. And. I just wanted to get away–it had been a difficult past fifteen months and I was tired and wanted to see new places and new faces.

Arriving at the Naturist Society office, I met Nicky Hoffman. We had been talking less than five minutes when she told we of this beautiful park that a couple, the Mitchells, had just bought near Union City, Michigan, with plans of converting it into a nudist resort.

Two days later, at the peak of the fall colors, I was back in Michigan touring Turtle Lake Resort, a beautiful 160 acre campground/resort, with owner Doug Mitchell as he was telling we of his and his wife Norma's plans to turn what had been a traditional campground into a clothing-optional growth center offering personal growth and self-discovery workshops and seminars within the safe environs of a nudist park.

Two weeks later, on November 1, 1993 1 started working as the newest member of the live-in staff at Turtle Lake Resort. My duties included public relations, conducting orientations and giving tours, with my compensation including being housed in a park-model mobile home over looking the beautiful Turtle Lake Lagoon.

The following week I wrote an article, "NUDISM: What's the Appeal?" which, unknowingly, would be a chapter for this book.

For the next year I would live a dream as I touched the lives of many people coming through the gates nudist park for their very first time. Seeing their change, I would, in turn, be touched–always adding to the sense of duty to write my book. Over this year, the first edition of this book would begin to unfold. I received more than I expected. DZ

Preface to
NAKED BEFORE GOD II

I am grandfather and a graduate of Wayne State University and a retired salaried employee of General Motors. I was brought up in traditional Christianity but my spiritual path has long since shifted toward Earth/Goddess and Nature-oriented types of spiritual practices.

Since retiring I have done a variety of activities including a year living in and working at a major nudist resort in Michigan, Turtle Lake Resort. My duties there included public relations, orientations for newcomers and guided tours. These duties afforded me the opportunity to take hundreds of people through the first-time nudist experience. It was during this period I wrote my first book NAKED BEFORE GOD: *A Look At Healing, Self-discovery and Spiritual Growth Through Social Nudism.*

I wrote that book not only to share my own healing experiences during the early period of me being a nudist but also to tell the stories of others who had their own unique, yet similar, positive and life-changing experiences.

Finding my childhood religious training extremely

limiting and oppressive, and seemingly being on a life-long spiritual path, I have since engaged in many practices and participated in many workshops and seminars all promising to raise consciousness leading toward enlightenment. And, they all did some good but I never felt any of them quite reached to the bottom, quite got to my core. None of them broke through—and I wasn't even sure at the time what they were supposed to break through, but none did. But then, doing something I thought was about as far from a spiritual path as one could get, I found nudism and something finally clicked. Something released. I was there. I felt I had come home. The feeling was profound. It took a long time to figure out exactly what happened but I knew I had found what I was looking for. Somehow, I had been validated.

I now feel that one of the most basic, if not the biggest issue to overcome on the way to higher consciousness, self-actualization, personal empowerment and just plain having fun at living, has to do with shame, embarrassment and guilt over our bodies *and their functions*. We walk around in a body that, from a very young age, most of us have learned to dislike. Then, realizing something is wrong with us but not having a clue as to what, we sign up for some magic seminar or workshop claiming to be able to raise our consciousness—spiritual or otherwise—expecting to get fixed, while completely unaware of our deep-seated body image issue. The most elementary and essential work of all is never even considered. No wonder most of these groups did little for me, or for many others, for that matter.

But, not only do they often fail in their claims because they don't address the most basic issue of body image, they often leave us feeling worse about ourselves for the program itself not having worked, that somehow we are flawed and that we need another session or the advanced course. The problem is that after taking them, we still don't like ourselves; we still don't enjoy ourselves at the physical level and that's where everything starts.

It's important to understand that spiritual or consciousness-raising practices (or any social systems or institutions, for that matter) that ignore or fail to recognize and honor our body and our sexuality, deny and degrade a basic and essential part of who we are and, for that reason, predictably fail. *Furthermore, by NOT addressing the problems of shame, embarrassment and guilt over our bodies and by not actually offering healing solutions, most of these programs actually perpetuate the problem.* So, without any awareness on our parts of their negative effects, they reinforce our poor body image based on the culturally-induced judgment that nakedness is immoral and shameful. Thus, they leave us worse off than before. If they are not part of the solution, they are part of the problem. For us to truly heal, we have to have the courage to face and break through this barrier.

The work I have done with my books, website and in

person, I feel, does just that. It addresses what most people know deep inside to be the truth about what they must do to *get free*. *"In our nakedness lies our freedom and strength."* -Daniel D.Ziegler

Introduction to the original
NAKED BEFORE GOD

THE HUMAN-POTENTIAL MOVEMENT offers hope for the human race. Perhaps more than anything else, the very existence of such a large movement demonstrates humankind's desire to survive, grow and evolve. With its millions of people involved in self-discovery, personal and spiritual growth, in its many facets, the human-potential movement offers hope of mankind's ultimate success in avoiding self-destruction and reaching an age of enlightenment.

As opposed to other periods in history, such as the age of scientific discovery or the industrial revolution, when mankind has looked outward for causes and solutions of its problems and answers to its questions, mankind is starting to direct the quest inward, toward self, thus beginning to accept responsibility for its present state of affairs as well as its future well-being. We are beginning to realize that perhaps the answers we seek lie within us.

As evidenced in our bookstores, there seems to be a shift occurring in which we are becoming interested not only in how to make a living, but also *how to live.* Whole sections of book stores are devoted to healing, self-help, self-discovery, recovery, new-age, spiritual growth, wellness, etc., indicating that wisdom and insight are becoming just as important to readers as knowledge and facts.

Perhaps the human-potential movement is evidence of mankind's readiness and willingness to learn how to get along with itself. Perhaps by going inward and learning about ourselves, we can and will learn about each other. Perhaps we will learn that we are not different and separate, but that we do indeed emerge from the same Essence and that only by truly loving ourselves, can we love each other.

Self-discovery and growth are as much about unlearning, though, as about learning who we are. Indeed, to grow we must shed many old ideas, concepts and attitudes that once served us but no longer work and, in fact, may hold us back. Healing, self-discovery, personal and spiritual growth have as much to do with letting go of the old as with recognizing and accepting the new.

This book is about a lifestyle that offers much in the way of healing, self-discovery and spiritual growth, most of which has to do with unlearning and letting go. It is about a practice that in terms of application and effectiveness can be compared to meditation–a mental exercise of letting go.

Anyone who has practiced meditation knows the powerful effect of clearing the mind. Relaxation, a heightened sense of well-being and often a greater awareness of our spiritual nature result. Group meditation often brings the added awareness of our spiritual connection to each other. The collective energy felt in a meditation circle can be unbelievable.

Nudity frees the body as meditation frees the *mind,* permitting us to be who we are. Being comfortable with private nudity requires a certain level of self-acceptance. Social nudity requires yet a higher level of self-acceptance, plus it offers us the added benefit of being unconditionally accepted by others. It allows us to relate to others without facades, pretentiousness or artificiality. The resulting sense of well-being is beyond comparison. As is meditation, nudism is one of the most powerful tools for healing, self-discovery and spiritual growth available to anyone.

Nudism is a lifestyle that, in and of itself, not only fulfills all the criteria of a growth experience but also serves as a beautiful metaphor. Indeed, the shedding of our clothes is a metaphor for shedding attitudes and perceptions that may no longer be needed or appropriate, while accepting our God-given bodies is symbolic of learning who we are at levels yet to be experienced.

Nudism has much to offer in the way of growth, but it is seldom thought of in those terms. Unfortunately, stemming from our society's puritanical views of the human body and sexuality, nudism is one of the least understood practices in our society–often falsely associated with promiscuous sexual behavior. Misconceptions, such as these, coupled with a general lack of reliable information, have kept nudism in the closet and out of consideration as a legitimate form of recreation, therapy or spiritual practice.

In spite of the relatively small numbers, nudism, also referred to as *'social nudism' or 'naturism,'* is actually one of the fastest growing movements in our country, and, according to a recent survey, nudism/naturism is the fastest growing segment of the tourism in the world today.

For lack of a better word, I often refer to nudism as a 'lifestyle.' It is a lifestyle for some, but for others it is only an occasional recreational practice, yet it touches each deeply because in the very act of participating, one moves beyond mainstream thinking to new personal frontiers. In these terms nudism is really an attitude.

But this book is not really about a lifestyle, it is about people, just as the human potential movement is about people. It is about people being healed, people growing, about people discovering, people experiencing, people remembering and mostly about people reclaiming acceptance of their original state.

Nudism. Have you ever wanted to try it? If you have, you're not perverted, and you're certainly not alone. There are millions of people, like you, who have fantasized about it, but so far have not taken the plunge. If an the other hand, you've never really given it much thought, you also are not alone. Millions simply don't know about it. This book is intended for all of you.

There are probably two reasons why more people haven't tried nudism: 1) There is a lack of good reliable information on what social nudism is all about and where to practice it, and, 2) The many misconceptions about what social nudism is, tend to scare people away before they even try it. In spite of its continued growth, nudism remains one of this country's best kept secrets.

This book is not intended to be a detailed or complete picture of the nudist lifestyle. It is, rather, glimpses, insights and experiences, by me and other nudists that will provide a safe and comfortable background on which you, the reader, can fill in the details of your picture with your very own experiences.

I will not attempt to provide you with a pattern or formula of how to experience nudism; as an individual, you will experience social nudism according to your own perceptions. Please keep in mind, though, that it may be so different from anything else you've experienced, that you may not yet have a framework on which to hang it. And it may take some time for you to process the experience and to interpret, describe or explain it, even to yourself. At first, you may just feel *'something,'* *'something'* you can't explain but *something* quite good. Enjoy it, that's quite enough, and take your time.

If you've ever read a self-help book, attended a seminar or workshop, been in recovery, seen a therapist, run a marathon, attended a twelve step meeting, had a massage, gone to a psychic, are a vegetarian, meditated or in some way been involved with one or more of the hundreds of activities associated with the human-potential movement, then this book is for you. It can assist you in your growth.

Whatever the reason you have picked up this book, it is not by accident. That I am writing these words and that you are reading them and that through these pages we have been brought together is by Divine order. Together perhaps we have already reached spiritual puberty and have begun to understand and accept who we are–spiritual beings having a physical experience.

To me and others, nudism has been a very powerful spiritual experience, touching us at the deepest level of our souls and leaving us changed from the first day we tried it. I hope this book will shed some light on this lifestyle that produces a major shift in consciousness in those that try it, and I hope this book will serve as a catalyst in encouraging you to make social nudism one of the next steps in your unfoldment allowing you to experience what we have felt.

If there is something in this book that speaks to you, listen to it, but more importantly listen to your own inner voice as it speaks to you. Free your body and your mind and LISTEN, as together we begin to understand and accept who we are. -Daniel D. Ziegler

Introduction to

NAKED BEFORE GOD II

NAKED BEFORE GOD II *is a compilation of my writings after the original NAKED BEFORE GOD was written in 1994. It roughly spans a period from 1996 to 2010 and consists of articles I published on various websites I maintained during that period, the most recent one called* Less-Ons For Truth. *The content of these articles revolves, more or less, around the topic of nudity and body acceptance but expands somewhat. The following paragraphs represent the Home Page from that site.*

I welcome you to LESS-ONS FOR TRUTH. We are like-minded individuals reclaiming acceptance of our original state of being, physically and spiritually. Rather than ignoring our bodies in the process of spiritual growth, we at *LESS-ONS* are exploring, experiencing and expressing, body acceptance and positive sexuality as a basis for self-discovery and spiritual growth.

Many of us have negative mental images of our

bodies and of our sexuality brought about by sexually repressive religious training during our early years or throughout our whole lives. These images are reinforced by Madison Avenue's and Hollywood's unrealistic and often contradictory messages of how we are supposed to look, feel and behave. When we can't live up to these expectations, we often feel flawed and unworthy. At *LESS-ONS For Truth*, we have come to understand that the healing of our shame, embarrassment and guilt over our bodies—and their functions—is a vital and essential, yet elementary, step in the process of self-discovery and personal growth. Through our healing we have thus come to know and celebrate the true beauty of our bodies and our sexuality.

Why the name *"LESS-ONS" For Truth*? The name is inspired by two completely different sources. The first is a *PhenomeNews* column by the hilarious Swami Beyondananda who humorously describes an ancient religious sect called Nuddhists. Supposedly followers of the prophet Nuddha, members of the sect traveled around the countryside teaching (mostly in the summertime) wearing nothing at all. Since they obviously had less on than most other folks, their teachings became known as 'less-ons.' The Swami surmises this may be the origin of the word 'morons' too. He also says, "And in a world where the 'More-ons' greatly out number the 'less-ons,' maybe this is a religion whose time has come." Perhaps the good Swami is right.

On a more serious note, the second inspiration for the name *LESS-ONS For Truth* is a wonderful book by Emilie Cade called *Lessons in Truth*. It is an inspirational and spiritual work that presents lessons in reclaiming our highest spiritual truth—our divine nature, which is our original state.

And so, I thought, why not *LESS-ONS For Truth (LOFT)*—like-minded people reclaiming acceptance of their original state, physically as well as spiritually? This includes people who: 1) Already know the 'naked truth' about themselves, i.e., are comfortable with their own nudity and sexuality; 2) Those who are curious and are seeking to know their 'naked truth' as an integral part of their overall self-discovery and personal growth process, and 3) Those who are in emotional pain and in serious need of body image healing work. A perfect name!

There is nothing to join to become a *LESS-ON.* You can just come on in and:

1) Casually explore the material presented here—and be yourself; or...

2) If something here touches you at the deepest level of your soul and nude living, nude recreation and even social nudism seem to be calling you, then follow your heart and try it. Nudism/naturism is about having fun. There is enough information within these pages to get you started ; OR...

27

3) If you have a poor body image based on the culturally induced judgment that nakedness is immoral and shameful and are in serious emotional pain yet you feel you are ready to be healed, however, you aren't quite sure how to go about the healing process, then read at least some of this material and contact us. There are many who have been exactly where you are in terms of poor body image who have found healing and relief from their pain. You can too!

Less-ons for Truth Mission:

Reclaiming Acceptance of our Original State

Less-ons for Truth Motto:

Ego sum sicut Deus me creavit. (I am as God created me).

Coming from the heart, Dan

Other than dividing this book into two parts, NAKED LESS-ONS and SEXY LESS-ONS, there is no particular order to the articles. They span a number of years and while some ideas are often repeated, change in thinking is also reflected. There is no recommended order in which to read these articles or chapters.

PART ONE

NAKED LESS-ONS

Chapter 1

SWIMMING LESSONS

In the summer of 1954, an eleven year old farm boy, who loved the water, desperately wanted to learn how to swim. Too many summers had gone by as the older boys swam in Squaconning Creek and the Saginaw River, while all he could do was splash around in the shallow water. He wanted to swim and dive off the bridge like the big kids. Attempts made by his father to teach him how to swim a couple years earlier failed as his impatient father deliberately dunked him several times. Crying and screaming but still wanting to learn, the young boy resolved never to ask his father again. Somehow he would learn on his own if he had to.

Through school, this fourth grader found out that the Red Cross was offering free swimming lessons at the big high school in town. However, because his mother didn't drive and his father was too busy from sunup to sundown with farming chores, transportation would be a problem. That problem actually had been solved a year earlier, however, when his older brother by three years, took the same swimming lessons and got there by riding his bike three miles into town, catching a city bus part way and walking the remaining seven blocks to the high school. A scary odyssey for very shy 11 year old, but one he was willing to face knowing that by the time he started in fifth grade next Fall, he would be good swimmer.

But there was one more catch—the biggest obstacle of all. He had learned from his older brother that the boys were required to shower together before the class—NAKED! That was scary!

Resolved to learn how to swim that summer, however, the scared yet brave boy filled out the registration card and mailed it in.

During the next couple weeks it was hard for the young boy to keep from thinking of the first time he would have to be in the shower naked with all those other boys. The fear was enough to keep him awake some nights but he kept thinking of how he would be the youngest kid to dive off the Church Bridge by the end of summer.

Accompanying him to the first lesson to show him how to ride the bus, where to get off and to show him how to get to the high school gym and pool, was his older brother. That made the traveling part easier to learn. But standing in line in the gym waiting to get into the locker room and shower was a different story. What was probably only a few minutes, seemed like hours. Finally, the moment came when a young man opened the door and led the boys into the locker area. Apparently sensing not only the nervousness of the shy farm boy but that of the other kids too, he calmly explained the showering procedure and reassured them it wouldn't be bad…and actually, it wasn't. It was the *anticipation* of it that was by far the worst part.

The young farm boy successfully completed the swimming lessons and, indeed, by the end of the summer of 1954 had become a competent enough swimmer to be the youngest kid to be diving of the Church Bridge on Ziegler Road.

But the memory of those anxious moments preceding the shower room would live on with the child for many years.

I grew up, married and raised a family.

Throughout the years, I had many typical encounters with nudity where it couldn't be avoided, such as high school swimming class, college dorm life and Army life. Though none of these was particularly difficult for me, it often seemed easier for others, and there was a part of me that didn't want it that way. I wanted it to be easy. As I thought about it over the years, I came to the conclusion that it *should* be easy. It was natural that we all have bodies and it should feel natural for us to be nude in the presence of others. Why it didn't for me or for many others, I would come to realize, is based on a long history religious and societal negative conditioning.

Although much within me had healed since those early childhood days of anxiety over the locker room shower, there was still much that needed to heal, and I set about continuing the healing process. I have written extensively about this in my book *NAKED BEFORE GOD: A Look at Healing, Self-discovery and Spiritual Growth Through Social Nudism*. The word that best describes the results of the healing is "freedom."

What I would like to add here is that I have learned that there are many people who, like myself, have had these negative childhood experiences with nudity but, unlike myself, as yet have not done anything about it—they have not healed. In fact, many times these memories have been stuffed way down, supposedly out of the way, and forgotten, yet they can still be influencing their lives in many ways. The good news is they, too, can be easily healed. That my experience as a shy eleven year old is still so vivid in my mind enables me to know that somewhere inside them, however deep it may be, there is a part of them that *could* be healed, that *wants* to be healed, that wants to be free. To be able to reach out to these people and know how to initiate the healing process is the gift I have received from this childhood experience. *I have learned that when that place is reached, ever so remotely, healing is possible, and the freedom definitely changes lives for the better*. I have seen it time after time. My book *NAKED BEFORE GOD* is one of the tools to accomplish that.

As I said, the *anticipation* over being seen nude in the shower room before the swimming lessons was by far the worst part of the experience for me. Once I realized I was alright and that nothing bad had or was going to happened to me, nudity became much easier. The healing had begun.

During the summer of 1954, in addition to learning how to swim and dive off the bridge, I added a bonus feat which may even have been more significant than the swimming itself. I went skinny-dipping for the first time— under the bridge, of course, and out of view of the church. Anyone who skinny-dipped as a child certainly remembers it, and while my memory of the shower room anxiety has slightly faded over the years, the feeling of freedom skinny-dipping hasn't.

Chapter 2

BODY ACCEPTANCE AND THE SPIRITUAL PATH

OUR SPIRITUAL PATH is the process of seeking self-acceptance at the highest level—the level of our spirit, our higher Self, our divinity. Spiritual awareness, then, is spiritual self-acceptance or acceptance at our highest level of existence.

The journey toward spiritual self-acceptance is preceded, however, by self-acceptance of our lower levels of existence—of our physical, emotional and mental bodies; and spiritual awareness is actually blocked if we hold negative judgments against these lower levels. Thus, negative judgments against our bodies, such as shame, embarrassment and disgust, are barriers to self-acceptance of our higher self.

The path to spiritual self-awareness, then, must begin at the very beginning—with body acceptance. Unfortunately in our society, we are bombarded from early age by negative messages about out bodies. Religion, entertainment, the advertising industry, as well as other sources, contribute to poor body image and a lack of self-esteem and self-acceptance. Before we even reach an age of self-awareness, we have already developed deeply ingrained negative attitudes that cloud our self-image.

Poor attitudes about our bodies not only block our path to spiritual awareness but also interfere with our health. By sending negative messages to our bodies and by mistreating them in the name of religion, fashion or whatever, we cause our own *dis-ease* and illness. Body acceptance, then, not only removes the barriers to spiritual self-acceptance and awareness but also removes the causes of many health problems. A body that is fully accepted and loved thus opens the pathway to spiritual self-acceptance and awareness as well as serving as a healthy physical statement of that spirit.

The Path To Body Acceptance

Many self-help books suggest that in order to improve our self-image we should stand naked in front of a mirror telling ourselves that we are beautiful. While this practice may, indeed, make it easier for us to stand naked in front of a mirror, it does very little to dispel the notion that our bodies do not fit within the normal range of bodies. That requires that we see other naked bodies.

Abraham Maslow, the famous psychologist, once made a statement to the effect that nudism—that is seeing other nude bodies—is a therapy in and of itself. Nothing is more healing to a poor body image than to see other real bodies because other real bodies seldom look like Madison Avenue would have us believe. Real bodies come in such a wide variation that it's not hard to dismiss the idea that we don't fit in anywhere. We will see that we do fit in.

To see real naked bodies is definitely therapeutic, but to to be seen naked by others is equally important and necessary. Being seen and accepted by others is the final step in learning to accept our own bodies. Once the negative judgments that stood as barriers to higher awareness are removed, we are healed of our negative body image, and we are now free to move to new levels of acceptance and awareness.

The path to body acceptance is often anticipated with a great deal of anxiety because it is thought that it may require years of painful therapy or some sort of traumatic psychological experience. Neither is true. The path to body acceptance is quickly accomplished—and is fun. Since nudity *is* our natural state, so *is* body acceptance our natural state. We are born with it, and we are simply returning to it; and since we have already been there, there is nothing new to learn. It is simply a remembering of something we've already experienced and is accomplished with great joy and freedom—and a sense of returning home. The path is *social nudism* or *nude recreation.*

Chapter 3

VESTURISM NO MORE

LET ME ADD a new word to your vocabulary and to the dictionary—*vesturism,* based on the word *vestures,* which *means clothing or apparel.* I define *vesturism* as*: prejudice based on whether or not one is wearing clothes.*

We already have the word *racism*, which is prejudice and discrimination based on race, and we have *sexism* which is prejudice and discrimination based on sex or gender, but until now we have not had a word for prejudice and discrimination based on the wearing or not wearing of clothing. Up until now this has not been a public issue, so we have not needed a word for this, but there is a growing movement now for clothes-free recreation and clothes-free living and a word is needed to describe those fighting against this movement.

This movement I am talking about is not just about nudists and naturists either. The nudists and naturists have their movements based on their organizations and beliefs and are pretty much content to stay in their private parks or otherwise designated areas. They seem to be operating alright and not really bothering anybody. We seldom hear about them. So the need for this word hasn't arisen from their activities, although many of them are involved.

The need for this word is based on a movement made up of people who feel they should have the right to be nude anywhere, anytime they please, even in public places. They call themselves **Body Freedom** and their numbers are growing. The participants in this movement feel they are being discriminated against by laws that mandate that clothing be worn outside private nudist parks or other legally designated areas. They feel that they should not be forced to segregate as such, hence the word *vesturism*—prejudice based on their not wearing clothes. (The word *nudism*, based on the word *nude* might be a better word here but, it is already taken with a different meaning.)

One might think that on the surface the idea of this word may seem a bit trite. I mean, come on, this doesn't carry the same weight as the words *racism* or *sexism* do, behind which we understand their significance, does it? *Vesturism*, come on, isn't that carrying it a little too far?

I posit that it is *not* carrying it too far and that we need to take a serious look at the issue of prejudice and discrimination based on the wearing or not wearing of clothing, because many of the same issues and reasons that made racism and sexism morally wrong are equally at work here.

Before we compare these issues, however, let me first say that the argument for clothes is often based on the highly questionable idea that people can be offended, shocked, and even psychologically damaged by seeing naked people. The concern is particularly intense with regard to children. The idea is that we must protect children from seeing nude bodies at least until age 18 (somehow designated as the age when it will no longer harm them). The truth is there is no proof that any damage actually occurs to adults OR children by being exposed to the nude body. The idea that nudity is harmful is not based on research but rather on preconceived ideas and learned behavior that have no logical or scientific basis. On the contrary, there is evidence, as the psychologist Abraham Maslow presented in his work in the 60's, that seeing and being in the presence of nude bodies promotes body-acceptance which promotes self-esteem and good health.

Now, as a comparison, let's take a look at our past history regarding racism. Prior to the civil rights movement in the early sixties (and prior to the word *racism*), many white people living in segregated areas of the south (but not exclusively in the South) felt that association with African American people (then called Negroes) was wrong and degrading, even harmful. Many whites certainly would not live in the black neighborhoods nor risk having their children suffer trauma by attending the same schools as black children. These were very strong beliefs, and political leaders such as George Wallace, as well as even some religious leaders, fought hard and were willing to put their lives on the line for their beliefs.

But we know that these beliefs were based on nothing but learned behavior. They ideas were simply passed down from one generation to the next, and there was no inherent substance to them. However, to those who fostered them there seemed to be. We now know they were largely based on ignorance and fear—fear of each other and fear of the unknown. It is a human trait to fear the unknown, and since we had not ever known a totally integrated society, we were afraid of it. Today, we see the fallacy of these beliefs, and all you have to do is look around in our schools to see how children of all races get along. While we still have room for improvement, things have changed. We live in a different world and are no longer afraid, and even many of the George Wallaces acknowledged that they were wrong.

A similar comparison can be used with the women suffrage and feminists movements. Today we know that many of the ideas and beliefs used to keep women down in the past no longer hold water. They were simply learned from those who came before us.

Many of our beliefs that are passed down to us from prior generations have strong roots, but that does not mean they are morally right or valid. To evolve as a species and to create a peaceful world we must be willing to look at our beliefs and continue to test them to find out which are false and holding us back, and then let those go.

We acknowledge intellectually that the human body is a marvelous creation. Yet we as a society still believe that if certain parts of it are exposed in public, it would destroy society. This is one of those beliefs that seems inherent in us but simply has been passed down to us and is now so firmly ingrained in our thinking that people actually feel they have been violated and traumatized if they see another human being nude. Well, there are probably many people still around who believe that society would tumble if our schools and the rest of society were integrated. They may still even believe that their children were irreparably harmed by attending school with children of other colors, but we know that did not happen. In fact, most would agree that we have a better society today.

In the same vain, there are many of us who believe public nudity would not cause our society to crumble. On the contrary, we believe, based on our experience and understanding of the human spirit, that simply being able to be ourselves, and not hide behind clothing, will lead to a higher levels of self-esteem and self-acceptance. This would lead to happier, healthier and more tolerant human beings *and* a better society.

So, let's take a serious look at vesturism and be honest with ourselves. Are we being vesturists, that is, are we irrationally discriminating against those who feel free enough to be themselves and not wear clothing? Or are we simply reacting irrationally out of fear of the unknown again?

As with the women suffrage, racial equality and feminist and LGBT movements, it will require a lot of brave people doing a lot of work before changes are made and we as a society overcome vesturism. But the work is already ongoing, and slowly things are changing again. I believe I will see in my lifetime when we will be able to walk down the streets of some cities and see a mix of people of both genders, of all races and religions, some wearing clothing and some not. We will look at each other no longer afraid and realize that, as with racism and sexism, our previous fears were unfounded. And we will look back and know that we have really progressed in making a better world by freeing ourselves from another irrational and harmful prejudice, from *vesturism*—a word that will not have meaning in our society.

Chapter 4

FEAR OF NUDITY

FEAR OF NUDITY, that is the fear being seen naked as well as well as the fear of seeing others naked, is among the most common fears we have and while it may be considered 'normal,' it is not natural. It is learned. Furthermore, it is among the most limiting of fears in that it prevents us from leading full lives, even though we seldom think of it that way. Let's look at its origins and then at how it limits us, and finally how to lessen the negative influence it has in our lives. First, however, I want to say a few words about fears and phobias in general.

Many fears, when experienced at normal and rational levels are self-protective mechanisms. Without them we would get ourselves in many dangerous situations. Fear of pain is an example. We wisely fear situations that may cause pain because pain usually means injury. These are fears with a healthy foundation. Fears that are unfounded, however, that is they are not linked to potential danger and are therefore considered irrational, often cause us to not lead fully productive and happy lives. Many of these fears are still considered 'normal' because most of us suffer from them. I say *suffer* because not only do they not serve to protect us, they, in fact, limit us, often in ways unthought of and unseen. Fortunately, the causes of these fears can often be identified and can quite easily be dealt with using proper techniques.

At the extreme and abnormal level, irrational fears are called phobias. Fear of nudity carried to extreme is called gymnophobia or nudophobia. Phobias can vary in degree of intensity and are often not only extremely limiting, but paralyzing to our lives. Even the thought of them can bring on terror or panic attacks. Phobias can have many different, and often unexplained causes and should be dealt with by qualified professionals. The fear of nudity I'm talking about in this discussion, however, although irrational to some degree, is still what we would call normal fear in that most of us have it but seldom does it cause us to panic. This fear is based on known causes and can be easily corrected.

Like many fears we are not born with, the fears of being seen naked or seeing others naked are not natural. As I said, they are learned. This can easily be demonstrated by watching young children. A two-year old just out of the bathtub is a free spirit whose spontaneous energy is difficult to contain. Many of us still have images of our children running around the house naked or even remember when we were allowed to do that. Then, usually somewhere around the ages between 2 and 5, the rules change as most parents begin to comply to the unwritten rules of society which dictate that we are to be clothed when in the presence of others. Thus begins the squelching of the free spirit and the beginnings of what later often becomes an unfounded and limiting fear.

Where do these rules about anti-nudity our society lives by come from? Traced back, we can see they come from western religion and such Biblical stories as the Garden of Eden and the story of Noah getting drunk and allowing his sons to see him naked. Whether we as individuals are religious or not, our western societies in general are highly influenced by these religious stories, and thus we as individuals learn we must comply or pay stiff penalties. Whether we consider these stories to be factual or mythical, they initially lead us to believe that social nudity is destructive and that if practiced, it will lead to the decay and destruction of morals and society in general. Is this all true? You decide if you want to believe all that but before you do, consider the fact that in this country alone we have literally hundreds of family nudist and naturist parks, camps and resorts operating peacefully with hundreds of thousands of people of all ages, creeds, sexual orientations all naked. Around the rest of the world there are countless places where social nudity is the norm. So much for the belief that social nudity is destructive.

So, what exactly is it that we are actually afraid of?

The answer is simple. If we are religious, it makes

sense that we are afraid of a vengeful God who forbids nudity. But if we are not religious, what are we afraid of? As I said, we are afraid that nudity will cause the destruction of sociey—*our* destruction. But, if it was really that simple, why are there so many staunchly religious people practicing nudity in our nudist parks and why are so many people in general so attracted to nudity that the advertising industry is able to exploit us by selling us merchandise using nudity? Are the religious nudists just weak people who can't remain "faithful," or are we really not all that afraid that nudity will cause our destruction? It doesn't seem that we are. No, there seems to be some sort of deeper understanding, even among the religious, that nudity is inherently natural and even healthy. So what is it, beyond religion, that we are *really* afraid of? The answer, surprisingly, is *each other* and *ourselves*.

Let's go back to the example of the child. Sometime usually after the age of two, the child, who up until that time has been free to be him or herself, learns that now he or she must remain clothed or face consequences. A few encounters with the rules of the society, even as enforced within his or her own home, soon teaches the child to comply or face the consequences of angry, or at least non-supportive parents. A few such encounters introduces the concepts of shame, embarrassment and guilt to the child, and it doesn't take many of these experiences before the age of innocence is passed and the 'normal' fear of nudity is deeply imprinted within the child. The child is now afraid of the consequences of nudity as imposed by *others* in charge. *A mechanism that will maintain a 24/7 conscious and unconscious lifetime vigil to see that he or she remains properly covered at all times has now been set into place;* but not only for oneself, the victim will expect others to comply as well, thus perpetuating the fear. That our naked bodies, once a source of joy as a child, have now become a source of shame, embarrassment and guilt as adults, can only lead us to the next step in our thinking: *Our bodies must be flawed.* Thus, we come to fear nudity because we fear the judgment of others as well as ourselves. What was once natural is now forbidden and disgusting, and the resulting unnatural fear is now so deeply ingrained within us it is considered normal.

How far we have strayed from our innocence!

How limiting is this fear of nudity in our lives? Perhaps more limiting that we think. Without thinking about it, in our society maintaining this vigil to always be properly covered becomes perhaps the number one priority in out lives next to survival. For the rest of our lives, with few exceptions, we will be required to comply, *or else*!

Chapter 5

JUST SHOW UP

"I'm not quite ready yet, okay? I need a little more time."

I've heard that many times before. I want to say, "No, you're afraid. You're afraid that something is going to happen to and you want to be ready for it. You feel more time is what you need, even if you have no idea what to do to prepare yourself during that time. You at least want to be ready to brace yourself so that if your emotions do begin fly apart, or whatever, you won't have a complete a breakdown."

I feel I need to address this issue. This is in reference to someone's intention to try nudism for the first time. Usually this comes from people who after several conversations with me, have come to the conclusion that this is something they need or want to do, either to heal from a poor body image issue they have been dealing with, or, less frequently, from people who simply want to try it as a fun thing and maybe have thought about it for a long time. But this second group seems to be ready almost right away. The sooner, the better. My comments here are mainly aimed at the first group who are in the majority.

The ones who realize they are in need of healing of body image issues are the ones who often feel they need to mentally prepare for the healing that will take place, that there is something they must do in order to minimize the trauma of some perhaps painful, serious healing experience. Being a totally new experience, they unconsciously may be comparing it to something they already know about or have heard about, such as getting ready for a bunggie jump or sky diving. These *are* big events that usually require some fairly intense mental or physical preparation and are events that tax their emotions frequently leaving them totally spent. And, even when totally prepared, they still brace them selves for it.

Therein lies the misconception. *It simply ain't that way here.* I have never seen anyone go through anything that even remotely resembles a traumatic emotional experience or is in any way physically or emotionally draining and has left them to recover in bed for days afterwards. It simply is not that way with this healing experience. Not even close. It's pure joy. Period!

Here is what happens. In the case of going to a nudist swimming event for the first time, any anxiety you have beforehand will begin to dissipate the minute you walk into the facility and see the first nude people. *Immediately* you will begin to feel a sense of calmness come over you. You can see that these people are nude and totally happy. There is not one ounce of anxiety in their body language or on their faces. These people are at peace, and you pick up on that immediately. You're already glad you came.

Then, while your left brain mental faculties are still thinking that seeing nude people is strange, your right brain immediately recognizes that there is something extremely natural about all this. A big part of you does not see it as strange at all. It's like something deep inside surfacing with the recognition that *this* is the way it was supposed to be all along. This is *natural*!

As you proceed to the locker area, you will see more nude people and each second that goes by brings this feeling of naturalness more to your awareness. At this point you already *want* to join them because that little inner you that has been held in so long knows this is the chance it's been waiting for, *and* seeing these other people has already given you permission to do that. That's all we need, permission.

And you go for a swim; you share a meal; you meet people; you talk to them. You see others interacting. You experience friendliness usually not found with complete strangers. There is definitely a sense of warmth there, and you recognize and appreciate it. You feel like family within minutes.

And so the evening goes on until it's time to dress and go home, and suddenly you realize it has been so relaxing that it is harder for you to put your clothes back on than it was to take them off. But you must dress, leave and return home.

You're home and you're thinking about the relaxing evening but also feel that nothing has changed about you. You're still the same person yet you expected something about you to be different by now. But there is nothing different. You're not spent, you not worn out. You need no recovery. You're just maybe a little hungry from being in the water for a good part of the evening. In fact, it's a little anticlimactic after thinking there would be more to it. You may even think disappointingly that you may not even be healed. "Maybe it didn't 'take' with me."

But it has.

You *have* changed. You *have* healed. You are *no longer* the same person. You no longer have to deal with these old issues. *But none of this has taken place visibly or perceptibly as you expected.* It's all happened quietly and without drama and without you even being aware of it. Not only did those changes occur, but these changes will be part of you the rest of your life whether you ever go back or not. This is the miracle!

The changes may not show up right away, or not in a few weeks, or months, but they will show up, and here's how. Sometime in the future you will find yourself in a situation which, for having had the nudist experience, you will react quite differently than you would have before that experience. *That* will be an "ah ha" moment for you, when you suddenly realize you are *far* different from before.

So, what you thought was a need to *get ready* or to *have more time to mentally prepare* or to *brace yourself* turns out to be nothing, *nothing at all,* completely unfounded. Part of you was expecting something on the order of a nervous breakdown and recovery. No such thing ever happened, nor will it.

So, how do you prepare? You don't. You *just show up* and the rest will happen ..and you don't even need to know how.

Life is a miracle. LIVE!

You're ready and you know it!

CHAPTER 6

DR SEUSS'S GIfT OF GOD

WITH THE DEATH of Dr. Seuss (Theodore S. Geisel) in September of 1991, the world lost a brilliant writer, and many of us feel that we also lost a good friend. Best known for his 41 children's books, he also wrote three adult books, two of those in his final years—*You're Only Old Once* and *Oh, the Places You'll Go!*. But few know that his first adult book, *The Seven Lady Godivas,** was published way back in 1939. It was not a success, however. It was reprinted in 1987 but failed again. In a letter to me, Dr. Seuss referred to it as a "failed publication." He wrote, " *...practically no one ever bothered to buy a copy."*

Today it is no longer in print and is only available through the rare book market. This article is an attempt to revive interest in the book by sharing an astonishing discovery about it.

In 1976, thirty-seven years after the publication of *The Seven Lady Godivas*, a work appeared on the market entitled, *A Course in Miracles,*** Published by the Foundation for Inner Peace, it had been written or, more appropriately, taken down through dictation of an inner voice heard by a professor of psychology, Dr. Helen Schucman. The voice claimed to be Jesus.

A Course in Miracles has been translated into a number of languages and has become the foundation for spiritual growth for many people around the world. It aims, in its own words, "...at removing the barriers to the awareness of love's presence."

In 1990, I discovered *The Seven Lady Godivas*. At the time, I had been working with *A Course in Miracles* for almost three years. I found *The Seven Lady Godivas* to be a delightfully humorous work that expressed a strong sense of physical self-acceptance and freedom to which I, as a nudist, easily related.

But there seemed to be more. From the very beginning, one phrase seemed to grab my attention. The words were, "Follow me." Dr. Seuss writes:

"Then she knocked at her sister's door. "Follow me," said Hedwig. Just that and nothing more."

In his brilliance, Dr. Seuss seems to deliberately draw attention to the words "*Follow me*" by adding, "*Just that and nothing more.*" "Follow me" jumped out at me, and I immediately thought of the references in the *New Testament* (KJV) in which Jesus used those words to call his disciples.

By this time, the book itself was beckoning me to follow it. After a number of readings, other passages caught my attention as well. One in particular, seemed to correspond to a passage from *A Course in Miracles* and another to a passage from the *Bible*. Upon closer examination, I was startled to discover that what was being revealed was that *The Seven Lady Godivas* contains a very profound spiritual message, and that the *Bible*, and more particularly, *A Course in Miracles,* are the keys to unlocking that message. The story seems to be a metaphor for our own spiritual journey.

This was an astonishing revelation to me, and I felt both a sense of elation and disbelief. Wondering, in fact, if what I was seeing was real or a product of my imagination, I shared my insight with a friend who was familiar with both works. She, too, was deeply moved by the uncanny connection.

Since that time, I have not been able to completely set *The Seven Lady Godivas* aside. The profundity of the message and the clarity with which *A Course in Miracles* reveals it still seems uncanny to me. And, since few copies of *The Seven Lady Godivas* have been purchased and even fewer by people familiar with *A Course in Miracles*, it has also occurred to me that perhaps I am the only one to have made this discovery. Thus, I feel compelled to write about it.

The following is an attempt to share, as I see it, the spiritual message within *The Seven Lady Godivas.*

The tale begins as Lord Godiva announces to his

seven daughters that he is leaving for the Battle of Hastings—by horseback. It is important to know that in 11th century Coventry, according to Dr. Seuss, the horse was still "experimental" and basically "remained a mystery." Lord Godiva doesn't even make it to the drawbridge before Nathan, his war horse, throws him "*spurs over breastplate off on his helm.*" By the time his daughters get to him, Lord Godiva is dead.

Saddened by their loss but recognizing their "grim obligation" to mankind to shed some light on the horse and make it "*safe for posterity,*" each Godiva sister swears that she will not marry until she has discovered a Horse Truth. Peeping Tom and his six brothers, to whom the Godiva sisters are engaged, await patiently as each girl pursues her Horse Truth Quest. As each discovers her Horse Truth, she is free once again to be reunited with her Peeping.

Through clever illustrations and witty writing, Dr. Seuss leads his readers through some hilarious experiences as each of the seven Lady Godivas follows her path toward discovery of a Horse Truth.

Laughing, the reader will relate to each of the girls as she is followed through her adventure. From one who says, "*I want another horse,*" we realize that we must deal with our issues as we have created them. From another we learn that being kicked in the rear can put us right where we need to be at times.

There could be much speculation about hidden

meaning in this wonderful tale, but to me the real significance of the story lies in its message of self-acceptance and freedom. Dr. Seuss describes the Godiva sisters' attitude as he writes:

"And their nakedness was not a thing of shame."

A sense of self-acceptance and its related freedom at the physical level is conveyed with these words.

But a strong sense of self-acceptance at the mental and emotional levels is also obvious. Each girl follows her own path and pursues her Horse Truth in her own way. One sister, analytical in her approach uses research to find her Horse Truth. Another says, *"I shall go at the horse from a nautical angle."*

That the book contains a spiritual message of self-acceptance is not quite so obvious, but nevertheless it is there. To unlock the message required me to allow my mind, in Dr. Seuss's words, *"to gallop wild along the most amazing thought lanes."* Doing so was quite an adventure for me.

As I stated, the words *"Follow me"* were the first hint I had of a spiritual quality to this book, and they invited me to look closer at other passages that might contain spiritual implications. I began thinking Dr. Seuss's beautiful words expressing Lord Godiva's thoughts as he observed his daughters. The words themselves seem to want special attention. Dr. Seuss writes:

"Nowhere, he thought with satisfaction, could there

be a group of young ladies that wasted less time upon frivol and froth. No fluffy duff primping, no feather, no fuss. They were simply themselves and chose not to disguise it."

That description, especially the last sentence, reminded me of the words from *A Course in Miracles*:

"*I am as God created me.*" (Lessons 94, 110, 162).

Although these words in *A Course in Miracles* refer to our higher self—our spirit—they aptly describe how the Godiva sisters must have felt about their bodies. It was possible, I thought, that the self-acceptance the girls felt about their physicality could be viewed as symbolic of how we are to view our spirituality. Yet that did not seem like enough evidence to conclude that the book carried a specific and intentional spiritual message.

The next passage to attract my attention first did so because it appears in italics. They are words spoken by Hedwig, the eldest daughter, as she instructs her sisters. As each discovers her Horse Truth, she is to inscribe it on a page in a special *Oath Book*, which Hedwig has prepared. Dr. Seuss writes:

"*So long as your page remains empty of Horse Truth, so shall your life remain empty of love.*"

After reading the book several times, these words seemed to inscribe themselves on my mind, demanding to be understood. At one point, as I was playing with them, I rephrased them to read, 'Find your Horse Truth and you will be free to love.' Then it hit me like a flash of light--

they were similar to words from the *Bible,* and I clearly saw them in front of me:

"And ye shall know the truth and the truth shall make you free," (John : 32)

The tingling that went through body and the tears that flooded my eyes told me that I had been given an important revelation. There was no doubt now that this book contained some very profound spiritual information.

But it still seemed to be in bits and pieces. Was this all there was—two seemingly unrelated passages? Or was there more? Did this book only contain fragments of spiritual teachings? Were the pieces ever going to fit together?

This is what I had so far: One passage that seemed similar to, *"I am as God created me,"* from *A Course in Miracles* and another that seemed similar to, *"And ye shall know the truth and the truth shall make you free,"* from the *Bible*. If there was a spiritual message of some sort, what was it saying? What is the truth that makes us free? Free to do what? Was it trying to say that if we discover our Truth, then we will be able to experience love, just as when the Godiva sisters discovered their Horse Truths they were free to be reunited with their lovers?

Whose love would we experience? These were all questions that were "galloping wild though my mind."

Several weeks later, I had the answers to these questions. One day, as I was cross-referencing between the

Bible and *A Course in Miracles*, I was led to the explanation of Lesson 110 of *A Course in Miracles* in the *Workbook for Students*. I could hardly believe what I was reading. At the top of the page read the words, "*I am as God created me,*" and toward the bottom of the page, as part of the explanation, "*This is the truth that comes to set you free.*"

As I read the words, I was overwhelmed with a sense of elation, and tears once again flooded my eyes. Not only was I totally convinced that the story contained a very definite and clear message, but here it was in front of me, explained in *A Course in Miracles*. What is the truth that makes us free, and what are we free to do? What is our Truth?

According to *A Course in Miracles*, our Highest Truth is that, in spirit, we remain as God created us—perfect in His image; and it is with this realization that we are free to experience God's perfect love. It is the highest level of self-acceptance and freedom. It is also the end of our Horse Truth Quest—the end of our spiritual journey. We have arrived.

Here then, totally expose, standing in all its glory, is the message contained within *The Seven Lady Godivas*: '*I AM AS GOD CREATED ME.*'

Although many spiritual works convey that ultimately self-acceptance and freedom occur at the spiritual level, *The Seven Lady Godivas* is unique in its approach in that it deals with all levels of self-acceptance, beginning with the physical. It serves as an important reminder that we must accept our physicality before we can accept our spirituality. Self-awareness and self-acceptance at the spiritual level are not possible until we have removed all the blocks and barriers that stand in our way at lower levels. Even negative feelings about our bodies are judgments that block our progress of spiritual growth. The Godiva sisters seem to be inviting all of us to reclaim acceptance of our original state—beginning with our bodies.

The Seven Lady Godivas is special to me. I wrote to Dr. Seuss several times, both to express my appreciation for the book and to offer my thoughts on it; and though he avoided answering any of my questions pertaining to the source of inspiration for the book, I'm so glad I took the time to write while he was still alive. In his letter to me he wrote:

"Thank you, Dan Ziegler, for finding qualities in The Seven Lady Godivas that are not apparent to the average reader.

"There are, of course no average readers of this book because practically no one ever bothered to buy a copy.

"Your letter and your review were greatly appreciated. They made me feel that maybe this failed publication wasn't a complete failure after all.

Dr. Seuss."

Was this beautiful metaphor divinely inspired, thirty-seven years earlier, by that same author as *A Course in Miracles*? Was Dr. Seuss aware that he was writing about our spiritual journey and expressing our ultimate Truth? What was going on in his mind as he wrote it?

Perhaps we will never know the answer to these questions and others, but that is not important. The importance lies with the message itself—with the fact that we once again have been reminded of our Highest Truth. Throughout history, mankind has been given this message often—often misunderstood, often misinterpreted, often forgotten—only to be revealed again. When we seem to have forgotten, we are once again reminded.

It is my hope that enough interest can be stimulated to revive *The Seven Lady Godivas* book and warrant a reprinting. After all, it wasn't written to be "a failed publication."

Translated, 'Godiva' means 'gift of God'. This book is a 'Godiva.'

* Seuss, Dr., *The Seven Lady Godivas*, Random House Publishing Company, 201 E. 50th Street, New York, NY 10032, 1987, ISBN 0-394-56269-0.
** *A Course in Miracles*, Foundation for Inner Peace, P.O.B. 1104 Glen Ellen, CA 95442.

Portions reprinted by permission from A Course in Miracles.

CHAPTER 7

THE EMPEROR REVISITED: By Hans Christian Andersen, with ending by Daniel D. Ziegler

MANY YEARS AGO, there lived an emperor who loved beautiful new clothes so much that he spent all his money on being finely dressed. His only interest was in going to the theater or riding about in his carriage where he could show off his new clothes. He had a different costume for every hour of the day. Indeed, where it was said of other kings that they were at court, it could only be said of him that he was in his dressing room.

One day two swindlers came to the Emperor's city. They said that they were weavers, claiming that they knew how to make the finest cloth imaginable. Not only were the colors and the patterns extraordinarily beautiful but, in addition, this material had the amazing property that it was to be invisible to anyone who was incompetent or stupid.

"It would be wonderful to have clothes made from that cloth," thought the Emperor. "Then I would know which of my men are unfit for their positions, and I'd also be able to tell clever people from stupid ones." So he immediately gave the two swindlers a great sum of money to weave their cloth for him.

They set up their looms and pretended to go to work, although there was nothing at all on the looms. They asked for the finest silk and the purest gold thread, all of which they hid away, continuing to work on the empty looms, often late into the night.

"I would really like to know how they are coming with the cloth!" thought the Emperor, but he was a bit uneasy when he recalled that anyone who was unfit for his position or stupid would not be able to see the material. Of course, he himself had nothing to fear, but still he decided to send someone else to see how the work was progressing.

"I'll send my honest old minister to the weavers," thought the Emperor. "He's the best one to see how the material is coming. He is very sensible, and no one is more worthy of his position than he."

So the good old minister went into the hall where the two swindlers sat working at their empty looms. "Goodness!" thought the old minister, opening his eyes wide. "I cannot see a thing!" But he did not say so.

The two swindlers invited him to step closer, asking him if it wasn't a beautiful design and if the colors weren't magnificent. They pointed to the empty loom, and the poor old minister opened his eyes wider and wider. He still could see nothing, for nothing was there. "Gracious" he thought. "Is it possible that I am stupid? I have never thought so. Am I unfit for my position? No one must know this. No, it will never do for me to say that I was unable to see the material."

"You aren't saying anything!" said one of the weavers.

"Oh, it is magnificent! The very best!" said the old minister, peering through his glasses. "This pattern and these colors! Yes, I'll tell the Emperor that I am very satisfied with it!"

"That makes us happy!" said the two weavers, and they called the colors and the unusual pattern by name. The old minister listened closely so that he would be able say the same things when he reported back to the Emperor, and that is exactly what he did.

The swindlers now asked for more money, more silk, and more gold thread, all of which they hid away. Then they continued to weave away as before on the empty looms.

The Emperor sent other officials as well to observe the weavers' progress. They too were startled when they saw nothing, and they too reported back to him how wonderful the material was, advising him to have it made into clothes that he could wear in a grand procession. The entire city was alive in praise of the cloth. "Magnifique! Nysseligt! Excellent!" they said, in all languages. The emperor awarded the swindlers with medals of honor, bestowing on each of them the title Lord Weaver.

The swindlers stayed up the entire night before the procession was to take place, burning more than sixteen candles. Everyone could see that they were in a great rush to finish the emperor's new clothes. They pretended to take the material from the looms. They cut in the air with large scissors. They sewed with needles but without any thread. Finally they announced, "Behold! The clothes are finished!"

The Emperor came to them with his most distinguished cavaliers. The two swindlers raised their arms as though they were holding something and said, "Just look at these trousers! Here is the jacket! This is the cloak!" and so forth. "They are as light as spider webs! You might think that you didn't have a thing on, but that is the good thing about them."

"Yes," said the cavaliers, but they couldn't see a thing, for nothing was there.

"Would his imperial majesty, if it please his grace, kindly remove his clothes." said the swindlers. "Then we will fit you with the new ones, here in front of the large mirror."

The Emperor took off all his clothes, and the swindlers pretended to dress him, piece by piece, with the new ones that were to be fitted. They took hold of his waist and pretended to tie something about him. It was the train. Then the emperor turned and looked into the mirror.

"Goodness, they suit you well! What a wonderful

fit!" they all said. "What a pattern! What colors! Such luxurious clothes!"

"The canopy to be carried above your majesty awaits outside," said the grandmaster of ceremonies.

"Yes, I am ready!" said the emperor. "Don't they fit well?" He turned once again toward the mirror, because it had to appear as though he were admiring himself in all his glory.

The chamberlains who were to carry the train held their hands just above the floor as if they were picking up the train. As they walked they pretended to hold the train high, for they could not let anyone notice that they could see nothing.

The Emperor walked beneath the beautiful canopy in the procession, and all the people in the street and in their windows said, "Goodness, the emperor's new clothes are incomparable! What a beautiful train on his jacket. What a perfect fit!" No one wanted it to be noticed that he could see nothing, for then it would be said that he was unfit for his position or that he was stupid. None of the emperor's clothes had ever before received such praise.

"But he doesn't have anything on!" said a small boy.

"Good Lord, let us hear the voice of an innocent child!" said the father and whispered to another what the child had said.

"A small child said that he doesn't have anything on!"

Finally, everyone was saying, "He doesn't have anything on!"

The Emperor shuddered, for he knew that they were right, but he thought, "The procession must go on!" He carried himself even more proudly, and the chamberlains walked along behind carrying the train that wasn't there.

Thus, we have the story of The Emperor's New Clothes *as told to us for many generations. But do not think for a moment the story ended there, for it did not. Ending it there would be a lie, a lie bigger than all the lies of the swindlers and of the Emperor's subjects. For generations, ending there has been a lie to cover yet another even bigger lie, the lie that the emperor had always believed about himself, and the lie that most of us believe about ourselves.*

THAT NIGHT THE EMPEROR was troubled and could not sleep, for he knew that he and his subjects had been made fools of by the swindlers. But he felt something else too, a wonderful lightness he had not felt before, "almost as light as a spider web," he thought to himself.

The next day he had his cavaliers chase down the swindlers and bring them to the courtyard where he had all his subjects gather.

"I have been a fool," the Emperor from beneath his canopy—still with nothing on—announced to a curious,

70

whispering crowd. "I have been a fool long before these two swindlers came to our city, but they helped me see my faulty ways."

As his subjects began to listen intently, he told them he now saw that his passion over new clothes was an attempt to hide from the shame and embarrassment he felt toward his body, and it was keeping him from his real duties as their emperor. "When I was supposed to be taking care of matters of the court, I was in my dressing room, obsessing over my new clothes," the Emperor said. "I was incompetent and stupid, for what I could not see was the magnificence of my own body."

"Yesterday, during the procession," he continued, "I suddenly overcame my embarrassment and shame, and I felt the freedom of no longer having to dress this body for concealment or adornment, of it being perfect just the way it is. It was a gift given to me by these two men who claim to be weavers. Indeed they are," he added, "yet what they wove for me was more precious than any clothes. They wove for me an occasion to be myself, just as I am; and their lies afforded me to see the biggest lie of all, the lie of fancy clothing behind which I was living." The crowd began to cheer.

"But I could not have seen any of this save the innocence of a small child who saw and told the truth," he continued, waving toward a small boy to come near his side. "I hereby bestow upon this boy the title of Lord

Truthsayer."

To a now jubilant crowd the emperor finished his proclamation. "Today, we honor these three Lords with another procession; and I invite all to walk with us, as I did yesterday, in all my glory, openly, honestly and proudly. And from this day forward, it will be said of me, your emperor, 'He attends to his duties, not fine clothes.'"

And everyone was happy, even the naked swindlers, and *especially* the wise Emperor who knew the innocent, small child would never have to know the shame with which *he* had once been burdened.

PART TWO

SEXY LESS-ONS

CHAPTER 8

BEYOND NUDISM: Sexuality as the Next Step to Healing

SOCIAL NUDISM CAN BE a healing balm for the soul weary of carrying around the burden of body shame. But at some point, if the weary soul senses a need for healing at yet a deeper level, the roots of body shame must be discovered and discarded. Only then will the healing process be complete.

What are the roots of body shame in our culture? When closely examined, shame, embarrassment and guilt over our bodies stem from thousands of years of religious-based sexual repression. We have been led to believe that our bodies are the cause of sexual behavior, most forms of which are considered sinful. It is this belief that lies at the bottom of our negative attitudes toward our bodies. To heal from this requires that a new understanding and appreciation of sex be adopted, one based on joy and celebration for life, not on shame and guilt. We can call it sexual acceptance. Simply put, sex must be brought up to an equal status as eating, praying, meditating or any other of a variety of normal nurturing activities of which we partake—openly, either alone or with others. Once achieved and we are no longer wasting vital energy concealing unnecessary embarrassment, shame and guilt, we will finally be free to pursue higher expressions of the human experience. Until then, we are slaves to our own negative thoughts of shameful bodies.

Just as importantly as healing our minds of the negative attitudes toward our sexuality is the next step toward healing of our body shame, comfort with nudity is a prerequisite for healing our attitudes toward sexuality. But it's important to understand that the healing of one depends on the healing of the other.

The whole process of healing begins with becoming comfortable enough with nudity to take the next step toward addressing sexuality. If one stops at simply nudity, however, the healing process will not become complete because body shame originates in repressed sexuality; and likewise, if one tries to heal his or her sexuality without first becoming comfortable with simple nudity, body shame will surely get in the way.

The two, nudity and sexuality, go hand in hand, yet, for obvious reasons, nudity must be dealt with first. We can even call that Step 1. Then, once a certain comfort level is reached with simple nudity, sexuality can be addressed as Step 2. After that, healing can be completed. The result is healthy sexuality based on an attitude of wholeness of the body that has replaced body shame based on sexual repression. We now experience true body acceptance that includes sexual acceptance, as we accept ourselves as healthy sexual beings.

I have written extensively about healing body shame through nudism in *NAKED BEFORE GOD: A Look at Healing, Self-discovery and Spiritual Growth Through Social Nudism*. It contains my personal experiences with nudism as well as accounts of other nudists and serves as a guide to the first step in healing.

For some, however, it will be the last step too, for they will choose not to explore the idea that their view of sexuality may not be entirely whole or healthy. For them, at least for now, a line has been drawn which they choose not to cross. Such socially accepted and mainstream concepts such as marriage, monogamy, heterosexuality, privacy surrounding sex, silence about sex, etc., etc., etc., are deeply rooted in our psyche and, for some people, are not open to be challenged.

Others, however, once they have experienced the healing power of nudism, will be ready for the second step, questioning society's and their own view on sexuality. Realizing that their body shame and possibly other neurotic issues originate from thousands of years of sexual repression, they begin. Their quest for further healing, however, will sometimes be painful as they move forward to challenge deep-rooted ideas at the very core of their soul—ideas even beyond the level of the nudism challenge—but the ultimate healing will be just as deep.

I have thought that since *NAKED BEFORE GOD* serves as a guide to Step 1, healing through nudity, I would have to write another book for Step 2, healing through sexuality. But after a little thought I realized that I would not have to write a single word. So much has already been written. One only has to go to a bookstore or look online for any number of books and websites dealing with healing our sexuality. With nudity, however, it was a different story. One is hard pressed to find any literature on nudity or nudism except what is published by various nudist and naturist organizations, and seldom does any of it mention healing.

I offer the ideas presented here to those nudists, and anyone else, who sense that even though the nudism experience has changed their lives in a positive direction by freeing them up from years of body shame, there is still something missing. I urge them to honor this feeling. That missing something, in my estimation, is the issue of our repressed sexuality. The nudist community, for a variety of reasons—some having to do with survival of the movement itself and some having to do purely with the blinding effects of sexual repression—has not addressed the *root* cause of body shame—our negative attitude toward our sexuality, It is up to us as individuals to continue on our own path of healing beyond nudism.

Chapter 9

AS WE ARE

CLOSELY RELATED to our need to express ourselves is the strong desire to *reveal* ourselves, and to be seen and accepted as we appear, as we are—naturally, honestly, without disguise. We wish to be accepted as we were born and presented to the world. Our presence is based on our individuality, on our uniqueness. We want to be ourselves, not having to pretend we are something else, and we want to be seen and accepted that way. To be able to do so is in many ways validation of our very existence. It is a simple desire yet it is a very deep desire, and it plays itself out in many ways—some acceptable, others not, depending on society's rules.

The desire on the part of social nudists to be nude in the presence of others, the desire of an exotic dancer or even a porn star to be sexual in front of the camera, the desire of a streaker to run nude through a public place and even the desire of an exhibitionist to flash a stranger, to some extent are all manifestations of this desire, that is, attempts to satisfy the desire to be seen and accepted as we truly are. Some of these are harmless acts, but others obviously are considered extreme and potentially harmful and threatening to others, yet for the most part they all are attempts to be seen and accepted as we are.

The problem with many of these acts is not that they cause any real harm to ourselves or others but that we are simply breaking the rules that our society has laid down for us. For the most part, the rules do not allow us to be ourselves, and when we act out on this desire to be ourselves, we are in violation of accepted or appropriate behavior. For example, according to societal rules, we are to cover ourselves and hide many of our natural functions, particularly those associated with our sex organs. The result is that we are either forced not to act on this desire to be seen and accepted as we are naturally are—naked—or if we do act on it, we must do so in violation of the rules and risk the consequences. This often is not an easy choice, especially for those who have a strong sense of who they are and a strong desire to express it.

Much of our energy* that could be used toward creativity or toward the genuine pursuit of happiness is misspent on our conscious and unconscious preoccupation with keeping ourselves covered. *It requires a great deal of energy to carry on a dual going on within us.* On the one hand, we are burdened with the shame, embarrassment and guilt resulting from society's rules imposed on us to keep our bodies covered and our sexuality hidden, and on the other hand, we have the natural inner desire to express ourselves naturally as we were created, to be seen and accepted as we are. This tug-of-war is constantly going on whether we are conscious of it or not, resulting in wasted energy that could be much better used in expressing ourselves as the magnificent beings we were created to be and solving our world's problems. What a waste!

I saw a bit on TV recently of a woman at a spa getting a massage for the first time. She admitted that she was a bit nervous beforehand, but claimed afterward that it was a totally relaxing experience for her. To me watching, it seemed to be a constant preoccupation and effort on her part to make sure the towel draping her was always in place. Her nervousness prior to the massage was probably based on her fear of being seen naked—a deep culturally-induced fear most people have. How could she totally surrender to the massage experience and enjoy it when her mind was really being distracted and she was focusing, consciously and unconsciously, on her shame and embarrassment? Although it may have been a somewhat pleasant experience for her, she missed the deeper experience by being trapped in culturally-induced shame, embarrassment and guilt—and she was undoubtedly not even aware of that.

The fear of being seen naked is a very common fear, and it is such a deep fear that it often enters our dreams.

Dreams have a way of revealing much of what unconsciously goes on in our minds during our waking state. This gives us an opportunity to become aware of it in order to process and reconcile it or work through these issues. Dreams of being naked in public places or among people we know are common, indicating buried fear. I even read results of a survey that showed that among many Christians, the fear of being naked on judgment day is a major fear.

So, how much of our lives are affected by this often unconscious fear of being naked? How much of our behavior is influenced by it? Probably more than we think. How would our lives be different if we didn't have this fear, if we weren't preoccupied with it? How much more could we accomplish if so much energy was not wasted in worrying about being covered properly? How much happier could we be if shame and embarrassment over our bodies were not a part of our lives? Probably a great deal.

I would like to go beyond the fear of nudity because I know that our fears of being naked are really based on another, deeper issue. Getting naked in the presence of others, as nudists do, is a step forward, but only a step. Merely getting naked, as nudists do, still leaves a deeper issue—the very issue that our fear of being naked is intimately based on and largely left untouched. It still leaves an unnecessary preoccupation with shame, embarrassment and guilt over our sexuality.

Largely as a result of western religion, we have a deep-seated fear of our sexuality. We are taught that this natural part of us is largely animal-like and must be curbed. It must be tightly controlled or it will get out of hand, resulting in a total breakdown of society. But the results of our repressing our sexuality in order to follow society's rules regarding it is that we have become a sexually frustrated society. Energy that should be expressed sexually—and there are many *healthy* ways of doing this safely—is instead being repressed; but like a stream of water that is being blocked, it will always find another way. Repressed sexual energy turns into misdirected energy and often displays itself in the form of perversion, depression, anger and violence and, of course, a preoccupation with what could be called 'junk sex.'

We all know that one of the things we must do in order to maintain healthy bodies is to eat good food. When we don't eat properly and get proper nutrition, such as when we eat a lot of junk food, our bodies cry out in cravings for what they are lacking. However, with junk food that is often lacking in the nutrients we need we pig out, eating way too much in an effort to get what the body is craving. But, of course, we never get it, but we get fat instead.

Such is the case with sex. When our healthy sexuality is repressed through social taboos, religious constrictions, social conventions, etc. and we aren't getting proper 'sexual nutrition,' we tend to pig out on 'junk sex.' That is what is happening in our society. Our obsession with incidents such as our leader having sex in the White House is an example of that, as is pornography** interest on the Internet.

The sad thing about being obsessed with junk sex is that we probably don't have much of a clue yet as to what healthy sex is or could be because we have never been allowed to experience it.

So, we wonder what's wrong with *us* and our violent society! But it's quite clear. While are we preoccupied with supposedly keeping our sexuality under control, our repressed sexual energy is manifesting itself in many other ways, including violence. *This* is what is destroying society—the very thing we were afraid of happening.

Must we be afraid of our sexuality? Is it something that left uncontrolled would destroy us?

No!

As nudists know, nudity does not destroy society as is often thought in mainstream thinking. In fact, nudist communities often have a stronger sense of family and community than non-nudists because nudity is our natural state, and it is in our natural state that we function in healthier ways. It would be no different with sexuality. Sexuality is our natural state, and if allowed to be displayed in healthy ways, much of our frustration, ill health and related dysfunctional behavior would cease to exist, leaving plenty of creative energy to solve the world's problems and pursue higher expressions of our human experience than we now know.

Presently, our televisions are allowed to show naked violence yet are not allowed to show naked 'love.' Our children are exposed to thousands of incidents of violence, including murder on, TV, yet never see people making love or even a mother nursing her baby. We have it backwards and thus we are creating the very kind of world that we fear.

If we could get over our fears and release the energy that is consumed in our preoccupation of concealing who we are, we could emerge into the magnificent, caring creations of who we are—something we don't even know yet.

I see a world in which we are neither burdened by shame of our bodies nor by fear of our sexuality, and we are free to seek the highest expression of our human experience.

*Wasted energy on our need to try to stay covered—a preoccupation with staying covered, it becomes a distraction, losing sight of what is really going
on.
**Porn—a desire to see ourselves as we are—sexual beings—looking at ourselves through others, vicarious living.

Chapter 10

OUR HEALING

IF WE LISTEN to the news and look at newspapers, we realize that we as a society obviously have problems. We seem to be a society out of control. Some say we have lost our morals. Others say we have forgotten God. Still others say greed has taken over or that our lives are too complicated, we need to simplify them. That we have a problem, we agree on. What we don't seem to be able to agree upon is what the real problem or problems are. Whatever the problem is, it shows up in many forms—anger, violence, rage and, all too often, in deadly shootings. It shows up everywhere—in our schools, in businesses, in government, in our homes, in churches, everywhere. There seems to be no group or situation that escapes its grip.

Deep inside, unconsciously, many of us know or sense what the problem is—at least a big part of it. But by the very sensitive nature of the problem itself, we are discouraged from admitting to it, from looking at it, and certainly from talking about it or suggesting what it might be for fear of being branded as being part of the problem itself. So we remain silent, and it remains an unmentionable. We go about our daily lives either ignoring it or looking for some other issue or issues to blame, kidding ourselves into thinking we can solve it some other way—fewer guns, perhaps more guns, tighter gun controls, and on and on and on. But we can't. These suggestions are simply scapegoats skirting the issue, and we won't solve the problem it until we have the courage to face it head on.

Perhaps it is in one of the ways that the problem shows up that is most telling or most revealing of itself. It is in the form of perverted and abusive sex. While this can be most revealing, it also is the most distracting clue too, for in these cases sex itself seems to be the culprit, or at least our handling, or mishandling, of sex. Yet this idea is misleading and without careful re-examination, we can be led down a path which can only make the problem worse, not better. So the real problem continues to elude most of us.

A few brave souls in our past know and have known what the problem is—or at least a major portion of it–and have been trying to do something about it for years. These are brave souls indeed, pioneers, in a sense, going where no man or woman in our society has gone before. But many of these individuals are not well known to the general public, and if they are, they are branded as being on the fringes of society, certainly not mainstream and certainly not people we would want to be seen or identified with. We won't see them at a White House conference on crime, for example.

So, what *is* the problem? The problem is simply our negative attitude toward our sexuality—not our sexuality, but *our negative attitude toward it*—and our resulting ignorance. The problem reaches every aspect of our lives, and the effects are more far reaching than any of us imagines.

Basically, we are a sexually frustrated society. We are a society operating on misdirected sexual energy. We are like a creative child whose creativity is stifled and whose repressed creative energy displays itself in frustration, in anger, violence and destruction. With that child, the creative energy shows its dark and shadowy side. So it is with our society.

Another way of looking at it is to think of someone who has poor eating habits, is not eating properly, therefore not getting their nutritional needs met. The body cries out trying to satisfy itself by pigging out on junk food which can lead to all kinds of problems—including behavioral. This is what is happening to us while we are pigging out on 'junk sex' while healthy sex is eluding us because of repression. The anger, violence, road rage, drug use, shootings that are so prevalent with us, are simply our repressed creative sexual energy showing up as frustration. We are experiencing our dark, ugly side because our light and healthy side has been repressed.

The most direct way this shows, of course, is sexual, in the form of perverted and abusive sex and our fascination and obsession with it. An example of this as an incident related to a former president is still all too fresh in our memories. Let us make no mistake about this, though, sexual repression rears its ugly head in many, many ways, not just sexual.

Another example is our general attitude of shame toward our bodies. We cover our bodies for concealment and adornment based on shame, and we have become obsessed with fashion to the point where teenagers are shooting each other over jackets and sneakers. The diet industry bombards us with often dangerous products, and women have dangerous breast implants inserted. All this is because we don't like our bodies, we don't like ourselves, which is ultimately based on our negative attitude toward our own sexuality. The problem of sexual repression is far reaching.

This is not startling new information, though. Freud and others have taught us about sexual energy, and what happens with us when we repress it. Wilhelm Reich, who wrote several books dealing with sexual repression including *The Mass Psychology of Fascism*, was thrown in prison where he eventually died for teaching that sexual energy is healing energy and could actually heal cancer.

This type of repression is still going on today, and any public figure who dares to speak out on the issue is quickly and quietly shoved back into the background. That's how deeply ingrained the problem is. An example of this occurred when Dr. Joycelyn Elders was fired from her post as Surgeon General of the United State for merely suggesting that we *talk about* masturbation in our schools as a way of curbing teenage pregnancies. Dr. Elders saw the problem and was sincere in her desire to offer positive solutions. She was onto something, *and most of us know that at some level.* But our shame, embarrassment, guilt, and, in general, our fear (or fears of our elected politicians) all lead us away from what would be a simple and healthy solution—or at least part of the solution—of a serious problem plaguing our society. Fortunately, Dr. Elders is still doing her brave work today, but she remains outside of the public sector. Our loss.

We are making some progress, though, but we still have a long ways to go. Today we are learning that Reich was correct. Sexual energy *is* creative energy, *is* life energy, *is* life itself. It is the most powerful energy there is, and if we try to smother it, it will show up some other way—*and show up it will!* And that is what is happening in our society, and that is what we need to learn.

Now, can we admit to that? If we can, how do we not have it manifest itself in negative ways? How do we let our sexuality play itself out in healthy ways? Aren't we talking about a sexual revolution with such ideas? All good and very important questions.

As a result of thousands of years of sexual repression through religious restrictions, social taboos, moral codes, emotional conventions, etc., it is difficult for of us to even know what healthy sexuality is, let alone how to let it play out. We are simply ignorant. All we know or all we have been taught—our entire attitude toward sexuality—is based on shame, embarrassment, guilt and fear. That cannot possibly be healthy, so healthy sexuality, for the most part, remains a mystery to us. We, as a society, probably don't yet have the slightest clue as to the beauty of human sexuality and how it can help lead us to spiritual enlightenment. But we need to start learning fast and stop fearing it, or it will destroy us.

The fear that we have of unleashing our sexuality is that, as a society, we would totally lose control if we were allowed to experience and express all our natural urges. What is happening, though, is that we *have* gone totally out of control as a result of repressing these natural urges. The very thing we feared is now occurring as a result of our fear, only in a different way. We are out of control with violence.

To correct the problem we must face our fear, that is, stop being ashamed of our sexuality, stop feeling embarrassed over feeling sexual, stop feeling guilty over being sexual and stop fearing our sexuality all together. If we can begin to feel good about our sexuality we will begin feeling good about ourselves. And why shouldn't we? After all, we were created as sexual beings, so to feel good about that, is to feel good about who we are; and when we can feel good about ourselves we will feel better toward each other.

Simply feeling good about our sexuality will go a long way toward healing many of our social ills. All we need to do is get in touch with ourselves, be ourselves, let ourselves out, and be all that we are. We all are simply crying to be let out. As creations of the Universe, all we want is to be seen and recognized for who and what we are, and that includes sexual beings. This won't require a sexual revolution, just an awakening. We would no more get out of control than a creative child gets out of control when handed a set of paints and paper or is exposed to music and begins to dance. A healthy expression and release of our sexual energy will remove the frustration that we now live with. It will allow us to feel good about ourselves, and it will allow us to re-channel much of that energy into many new forms of creative social endeavor that will genuinely improve social conditions on the planet. We will not lose control, as we have feared, we will gain control.

But how do we begin? By first being willing to look at ourselves, recognizing that our attitude toward our sexuality might just be a major problem, that it just may be the cause of what is going on in our society. This will probably be a most difficult step to take, however, because we are in such denial over the whole issue of our sexuality.

The ingraining runs very deep and, like all denials, covers its own tracks. But if we are to save ourselves from self-destruction, we must begin by recognizing and admitting our mistake.

Then, we need to actually get in touch with our sexuality. This may not be easy either because we have never truly done that. We have never truly accepted our sexuality as something healthy and beautiful. Therefore, we may not be able to overcome all the shame, embarrassment, guilt and fear in our lifetime, but we can at least begin, thus leaving the door open for our children to break the cycle we have been trapped in.

To get in touch with our sexuality, we need to step out of our comfort zone and learn of sexuality anew. We can begin by reading books on sexuality—even erotica. There are many good books in our bookstores, and many books on spirituality include discussions of positive sexuality. One of the pioneers I refer to is Betty Dodson PhD, sex educator and author of *SEX FOR ONE* and *ORGASMS FOR TWO*. I highly recommend these. The Internet, in spite of its reputation for containing pornography, contains a wealth of good information. There are many excellent web sites dedicated to positive human sexuality, and there are many excellent books and videos available through these sites. A good site is the *Society for Human Sexuality*. Much of this information is provided by those whom I mentioned earlier—the pioneers—who work on the fringes of our society doing the ground work in human sexuality. They are the ones who recognize that we have serious problems in the area of our sexuality, and they are the real experts on the subject.

Then, we can attend lectures and seminars. Start discussion groups—even in our churches—where there may be the most opposition but where they are most needed. Share with others the material that we have. Talk openly with others, and share what we've learned—and what we're feeling. Best of all, learn about ourselves. This is *so* important. Learn to like ourselves, learn to love ourselves and most importantly, learn to *make love* to ourselves totally in touch with how that feels, and feel good about doing that. That is an important step because self-love is the beginning of all love.

And the last thing we need to do, but certainly not the least important, is to teach our children to love themselves and their sexuality—no shame, no embarrassment, no guilt, no fear—just to love themselves, as Dr. Elders was suggesting. Our teenage children need a healthy, safe release of their sexual energy, and they need and deserve our support and encouragement in doing so, after all, they are sexual beings too. Again, this may not be an easy step for us, especially since we have pushed the job of sex education off on to our schools because we were afraid to talk about it ourselves—or didn't know enough about it. Again, the shame and embarrassment runs deep, but let's not pass as much of it on to our children as was passed on to us. Rather, let us teach them love, beginning with self-love. An excellent book in this area is HARMFUL TO MINORS: *The Perils of Protecting Children from Sex* by Judith Levine.

All these steps will all serve as a beginning. Since we are products of sexual repression, we have no clear guidelines to go by, so much of what we will learn will be discovered as we go along. But if we can constantly remind ourselves to always come from love and never from fear, we will be guided through this uncharted territory to our destination.

In conclusion, it would serve us well to be honest with ourselves over this whole issue and admit we know what the problem is. If we can, we will have made great strides into healing the human psyche and the planet. We may, indeed, even be saving ourselves. To look at ourselves honestly is perhaps the most difficult part but also the most rewarding. We must then trust this process, and if we can trust the process, the rest will follow. The next generation can live more peaceful lives and can enjoy what we most feared—our own God-given sexuality. Let us be the ones who discover that our sexuality can indeed lead us to enlightenment. And, let's not forget to have fun.

I see a world in which we are neither burdened by shame of our bodies nor fear of our sexuality, thsu, free to seek the highest expression of our human experience.

Chapter 11

NUDISM AND SEXUAL REPRESSION

I REALIZE NOW, some years after writing my book NAKED BEFORE GOD: *A Look at Healing, Self-discovery and Spiritual Growth Through Social Nudism*, that my claim that participating in organized nudism can increase body awareness and self-acceptance may not be as true as I once thought. While social nudity itself—that is, being nude in the presence of others—can certainly increase body acceptance, organized nudism as we know it in this country has major flaws that I now think may actually have a negative effect on self-esteem. This article is an attempt to explain this idea.

By not permitting any open display or expression of sexuality, the nudism movement reinforces our society's already negative attitude toward sexuality and, therefore, toward our overall self-image. In this respect, the organized movement is actually counter-productive to its claims. They need to quit making that claim or change the rules.

A while back, I received a phone call from a man

97

who, with his wife, had visited a nudist park for the first time. There, he had met a friend of mine with whom he got into a discussion about nudism. Being new to it, he had a lot of questions and was making a lot of observations about the nudist lifestyle as he was seeing it for the first time and about people's behavior under these, until-now unusual conditions. Wanting to be as helpful as possible in explaining the lifestyle, my friend mentioned my name and that I had written a book about nudism. His call was to see how he could acquire the book and to ask me a few questions concerning him and his experience.

Basically, what he expressed to me was that he had been very uncomfortable at the park. He had gone through the normal orientation that they required for newcomers in which he was told a number of things, including how comfortable and relaxing nudism is, that it is not sexual, and, in fact, no outward form of sexual expression would be tolerated. To further explain this, nudist park owners usually tell men that "if you should become 'aroused,' cover yourself with your towel or put on a pair of shorts, or you will be asked to leave."

He found the park and surroundings very beautiful and the naked people generally friendly, and all this is what contributed to his being uncomfortable. He found the whole situation—the sights, the sounds, the smells—so stimulating that he had an erection most of the time he was there and, therefore, was forced to wear a pair of shorts the whole weekend. "It was awful," he said to me, "I could not be myself. I never want to go through another weekend like that again."

I had very little to offer him at that point except my usual pitch that I had used when I was the one giving the orientations at that very same park. I told him not to give up on nudism, that he would get used to the nudity and that soon he would not find it overly stimulating and arousing. "You won't even get a hard-on," I said.

That phone call prompted me to begin to examine my own personal experience with organized nudism and to ultimately change my views about it—hence this article. What I told him was, in fact, what I had done to myself. In my attempt to set an example for others and to not feel guilty for feeling sexual myself, I had repressed my own sexual urges at the park to the extent that I was lying to myself about what I was feeling. What I really wanted to do was to be myself and let everyone know that I was a healthy sexual person—and that is what he wanted and I believe what most everyone wants.

To permit nudity yet not allow *any* form of sexual expression, not even an erection, seems like a cruel tease at best and an impossibility at worst. Either way, it is a form or sexual repression. The nudists' claim that nudism is not about sex and that nudist parks are in no way sexual is hypocritical. The very nature of nudity in an otherwise clothed society is certainly going to increase sexual awareness. To not be able to express that in any way, not even in touching ourselves or getting aroused, is simply unrealistic *and* cruel. And so, when we fail at this, even if just in our thoughts, we consciously or unconsciously feel increased guilt, shame and embarrassment over our sexuality, which merely adds to our already societally-induced poor self-image problem in general.

We are sexual beings, and our sexual energy will manifest itself one way or another no matter how hard we try to discourage it. If we can't express it in an open and positive manner, it will cause us to act out in unhealthy ways such as aggression or substance abuse. The nudists— the unsuspecting victims of this sexual repression—seem to have various ways of displaying their behavior and of coping with the dilemma of being torn between freedom that they know they could feel and repression that they actually do feel. Many do what the rest of society does either numb themselves with substances such as alcohol or act on their sexual feelings and lie about it. Some, to the dismay of the owners of the so-called "family nudist parks," no longer even lie about it. They are known as swingers, and they are out there in numbers; but in spite of how we might characterize or judge their lifestyle, they are the honest ones.

The nudist organizations themselves are not to be heavily blamed for contributing to sexual repression, however. They, after all, are simply extensions of our

100

western society that for centuries has repressed human sexuality, and they have had to conform to present standards in order to survive at all. We at least need to give them credit for attempting to defy some of the rules of society and break free from the pack.

If we are to ever become the enlightened society we are capable of being, we need to further free ourselves from the social restrictions and religious taboos that have forced our sexual energy to manifest itself in destructive ways. We need to learn to trust our sexuality, to fully express it, and learn that to be free with it does not mean we are going destroy ourselves. In fact, by repressing it we are destroying ourselves. Rather, being free with it means that we can channel it into creative expressions such as helping each other and saving the planet. Only when we fully accept and respect ourselves as sexual beings will we truly see ourselves as more than that—spiritual beings having a sexual experience. That is the highest form of self-acceptance there is.

I now have nudist friends who are not only comfortable with their bodies but with their sexuality as well. We associate outside the park in our homes, etc. We feel comfortable to be ourselves and do not hide our sexuality from each other. In fact, we honor and celebrate it. The tension and discomfort that the gentleman referred to in his phone call are not there. *It is relaxing because it is self-acceptance.*

Chapter 12

SEX, GOD AND ET'S

WHETHER WE ARE AWARE of it or not, we in the western world live under severe sexual repression due to socially imposed religious moral codes. Therefore, most of us have fairly negative attitudes toward our sexuality. Even if we don't consider ourselves to be religious or sexually repressed, we still are under the influence of these codes because they mold our society. A clear example of this is our laws requiring us to wear clothing. As a result, for the most part, we live in a constant state of embarrassment, shame and guilt over our sexuality (and our bodies in general). In the presence of others, we pretend to be asexual, that is, we hide our sex lives and we are uncomfortable talking about our sex lives in most circles—especially to our parents and children—and, in general, treat sex as something private at best and evil and dirty at worst.

The effects of this sexual repression are deeply ingrained in us. Wilhelm Reich devoted much of his life's work to showing the devastating effects of repressed sexuality in the form of neuroses in individual lives as well as in the form of oppression at the societal level. Several of his books including *The Function of the Orgasm* and *The Mass Psychology of Fascism* are devoted to these topics and are definitely worth reading. It is clear from his work and worth remembering that how we see ourselves and how we react to the world around us are both heavily influenced by our conscious and unconscious sex-negative attitudes stemming from sexual repression. It is refreshing to see, however, that at least some attempts are being made by some community groups, such as Seattle Washington's Sex Positive Community Center, to create and provide a positive environment for people to learn and interact with others in sex-positive ways.

As a society or as individuals, we will not completely be free of these imposed religious moral codes or change our attitudes about sex until we change our old fearful religious conception of God, for it is the deeply ingrained and often unconscious fear of God that restricts much of our sexual behavior. And we will not change our fearful conception of God until we increase our understanding of many of the ancient religious texts, particularly the *Old Testament*, which seem to speak of a God full of wrath and eager to punish.

Based on the works of Zecharia Sitchin and others, we can begin to re-examine these ancient religious texts in a new light—as records of extraterrestrial influence on early civilizations. This is not a new idea, but it is one whose time has come in light of mounting evidence of UFO's, extraterrestrial life and of ancient extraterrestrial influence on humanity's origins as well as on the mounting evidence of subsequent and obvious cover-up of such information. We have been led to believe that documents such as the *Old Testament* of the *Bible* are a record of "God's" work on earth. The truth is it is not "God" but oppressive extraterrestrial beings posing as God or gods and attempting to control us of which the texts speak. It is this misunderstanding of events described in these early text that has led us to our present religious concept of a vengeful and wrathful God who punishes us for enjoying "pleasures of the flesh" and forms many of our present limiting belief systems.

Research into these texts now clearly shows them to be records of extraterrestrial visitations and activities. They tell of ancient astronauts, technically more advanced than we, who visited earth hundreds of thousands of years ago and "created" (today we would say genetically engineered) humankind as a slave race. As one of the methods to control us, they forced unnatural and unreasonable restrictions on our sexual activity. This predictably produced frustration, poor self-esteem and all sorts of dysfunctional behavior, including violence among ourselves, as can be inferred from Reich's work. That is how they managed to oppress and control us for their purposes. Their negative influence deeply affects our thinking and behavior yet today.

In order for us to evolve into the magnificent, loving, and, yes, sex-positive creatures we are capable of becoming we must discard our beliefs based on old interpretations of these texts and form new beliefs. Coming to this new understanding of ancient religious texts forces us to confront and challenge some of the most basic moral and religious precepts upon which modern life in the western world is based.This includes our government's official position that there is no evidence of extraterrestrial life. If we are to save ourselves from self-destruction, if we ever to evolve into enlightened beings and experience a golden age—an age free from hate and violence—we must confront these issues *now* before it is too late.

We can begin doing this by first considering that our old paradigms may no longer be valid if, indeed, they ever were, and continue by seeking new ways of looking at our world and ourselves being one. We must also come to understand God, or Creative Intelligence, Source or whatever one wants to call the Universal Creative Force as a God of love and creativity, not of wrath and destruction, When we do this, we will see that human sexuality, in its *many* expressions, is a gift to be enjoyed and celebrated. Then, we must build a society based on our new concept of loving ourselves and loving—not fearing—each other.

It is evident to many of us that a God that creates

life through sex and creates us as highly sexual beings intends us—*all of us*—to enjoy sex and to use sex to celebrate life itself. It is this self-perpetuating characteristic of sex that demonstrates its grandeur and suggests that it is of the highest order of magnitude and magnificence of all creations. It is an expression of life itself. To hide it, to unnaturally restrict it, to misuse it or to be embarrassed about it, is to degrade it and to degrade life, and even worse, to degrade the Creative Force.

There is one final step in the progression definitely worth contemplation. I mentioned at the beginning that the work of Wilhelm Reich clearly points out how we see ourselves and how we react to the world around us are clearly influenced by our conscious and unconscious negative attitudes toward our sexuality stemming from repression. It is further suggested by one writer of UFO and related material, Michael Mannion, that the view of some modern extraterrestrials, presented by some contactees/abductees, as being uncaring, unloving and asexual may, indeed, be a reflection of our own sexual repression. If this is the case, how does this all tie together? Clearly, then, our thinking seems to be trapped in a closed circle which may be holding us back from entering the cosmic era. Misinterpretation of ancient documents describing ancient extraterrestrial activity forms our present misconception of God which, in turn, forms our outmoded view of sex which, in turn, influences our present view of some modern ET's who may be attempting to interact with us in friendly ways.

It goes without saying, then, that before we can objectively understand and intelligently interact with beings more advanced, it is imperative that we somehow break this negative cycle, clean up our violent tendencies and get our thinking straight about how to get along with each other. Then and only then will we be able to advance ourselves as a race of magnificent and sensual beings ready to join other beings in this cosmic era and possible golden age.

Do we have a good reason, then, to examine our present attitudes and ideas about our sexuality and make efforts to heal from the embarrassment, shame and guilt most of us live with? I think so!

For further reading on extraterrestrial influence on humanity and religion, one might begin with *GODS, GENES, AND CONSCIOUSNESS* by Paul Von Ward, *PROJECT MINDSHIFT* by Michael Mannion, *THE GODS OF EDEN* by William Bramley, *HUMANITY'S EXTRATERRESTRIAL ORIGINS* by Arthur David Horn and *THE EARTH CHRONICLE* series by Zecharia Sitchen. For reading about the connection between violence and sexual repression, in addition to the above mentioned books by Wilhelm Reich, see SAHARASIA: *The 4000 BCE Origins Of Child Abuse, Sex-Repression, Warfare And*

Social Violence, In The Deserts Of The Old World by James DeMeo.

Chapter 13

THE HUMAN SEXUAL EXPERIENCE
By Pazzi Wan*

YOU OFTEN SPEAK of yourselves as "spiritual beings having a human experience," and while this is true, you would be more accurate in your thinking if you referred to yourselves as 'spiritual beings having a *sexual* experience.'

Consider the possibility that sexuality is the main reason for the human experience, the reason spiritual beings, in general, incarnate in human form. Remember, without physicality, spirit cannot experience the sex act so taking on a physical body is necessary for this. Think about it: You come into the physical world as a result of the sexual act and you procreate through the very same act. Nothing speaks more clearly to the magnificence of human sexuality than the fact that it is used to create human life. It reasonably follows, then, that a major reason for the human experience is to experience the magnificence of sexuality. When you get this, you will stop degrading the sexual experience and you will begin to experience and enjoy it much differently.

Because it is what you came here to experience, sexuality will always continue to be a dominant part of your lives as it is now, but when you begin to see it in a more positive way, you will no longer let it control you. If you don't think it controls you now, look around you. It controls virtually every aspect of your lives. You are obsessed with sex, either trying to promote it or prevent it. The advertising industry is just one example of promoting it. Your most successful (and often most harmful) products contain and are sold to you through sex appeal. Your television is one of the media used for this, yet on this same TV you are not permitted to view a mother nursing her baby because the bare breast is associated with sex. This is an example your efforts to prevent sex. Yes, it controls you.

The problem is you have a negative attitude toward sexuality, therefore, your sex controls you in negative ways. You are experiencing the dark and shadowy side of your sexuality which is often fosters anger, frustration, low self-esteem, violence and even illness.

Now, when you finally accept that the reason you came here in the first place is to experience sexuality, you will look at it much differently. You will see it as a gift to experience as pleasure and joy. It will continue to be a dominant force in your lives, as it does now—because that is the very reason you came here—but you will be in control of it. This will allow you to experience it in positive ways and evolve through it in its many layers—from purely physical to highly spiritual.

This will come about when you are allowed to begin your experience with your sexuality *as children* and as you are taught *early on* to appreciate and to enjoy it. One thing you will be taught and encouraged to do, is to masturbate. Masturbation is a *fundamental* sex act and it is the *primary* sex act since it is your first experience with your sexuality. A new attitude toward this practice is what will keep sex from being expressed as a violent outburst of frustration and anger as it so often is done now among your young people. Obviously it will prevent unwanted pregnancies as well. A healthy, positive attitude and practice of masturbation even in, and *especially* in, relationships will keep sex in the proper perspective throughout all your lives since much of the frustration, anger and low self-esteem associated with your sex drive now will no longer exist. This new attitude toward masturbation in particular and your sexuality in general will go a long way in curing many of your social ills.

Throughout your lives you will experience the many facets or layers of sexuality, from purely physical to highly spiritual, from self-love to loving another; and you will take as long as you want—as many lifetimes as you need—to feel complete in the sexual experience. Having done that, your soul will choose to move on to bring yet another new experience to your Divine Creator. Until then, you are human beings, yes, but more—*you are spiritual beings*

having sexual experiences.
    Enjoy and celebrate!

•Pazzi Wan can be thought of as a being from elswhere observing the Earth.

Chapter 14

THE GIFT OF SEX
By Pazzi Wan*

Your view of your sexuality in your culture is clouded by shame, embarrassment and guilt resulting from centuries of negative influence by political/religious institutions that have a vested interest in how you think and behave. And because of your limited view, your expression of your sexuality is dark and distorted, often driven by frustration and anger and consisting of secret, hurried, clandestine and sometimes violent acts having little or nothing to do with love of one another or love of yourselves.

The effects of your negative attitude toward your sexuality are far greater than any of you imagine and they encompass virtually every aspect of your lives, thus preventing you from realizing your full human potential—both individually and culturally.

As you begin to realize that your attitude toward your sexuality is shrouded in shame, embarrassment and guilt, you will begin to see that this attitude stems from your view of God; and you will realize that your view of God must necessarily also be clouded as well—clouded in fear. You will see that this fear of God has been imposed on you by the religious institutions that have implemented rules, restrictions and moral codes that have limited you in your sexual behavior and expression—and, indeed, in your entire range of human experience.

But, could an all-loving God have given you something so wonderful as sex and then restricted its expression through rules and laws that are virtually impossible to keep? And, would It then punish you for violating those rules? Can God be both that loving and that cruel? Of course not. But there are, indeed, other outside influences, literally from other worlds, behind your religious institutions that have distorted your concept of God for their purposes.

A correction of your thinking will come from nothing less than complete questioning of your old teachings and beliefs of God, and this will eventually lead to a complete paradigm shift—a shift from your old fearful view of God to a new and trusting one.

You can begin examining these old teachings, along with their origins, by looking outside of your own particular scriptures and examining the writings that predate them. Learn of the very identities of the sources of these teachings and their motives and thus question everything you have been taught about God. Finally, challenge all you've ever learned about your sexuality.

Only complete questioning of the old paradigm will enable you to escape its negative influence.

Once your old belief system has been found out dated and is set aside giving you the freedom to determine your new beliefs and practices based on your *own* experiences, a new and fresh concept of an all-loving, non-judgmental God will emerge. This concept will include an understanding, indeed, an appreciation, that your sexuality is a gift from God, and that as your body/spirit connection, your sexuality is meant to be exercised, enjoyed, even celebrated. This healthier attitude and expression of your sexuality, along with your newfound view of an all-loving God, will lead you, then, to the fullest expression of your true human potential.

One final and necessary step remains—forgiveness— the recognition that this whole process has been a gift from those whom you thought controlled you; that God's understanding of the final outcome--your growth as well as theirs—was the reason the whole process was initiated in the first place.

A celebration is in order.

•Pazzi Wan can be thought of as a being from elswhere observing the Earth.

Chapter 15

THE SHAPE OF THINGS TO COME

HAVE YOU EVER LOOKED closely at a penis, I mean *really* looked at it, studied it? If we allow ourselves to get past the embarrassment, shame, guilt and judgment connected with our sexuality that sometimes prevents us from taking a close look at such things, we see that the shape of the penis is truly fascinating—particularly, the glans or the head; and not just the penis, but the tip of the clitoris as well. They are very similar—the clitoris is just smaller and more difficult to see. The shape of the penis is absolutely amazing, compelling even alluring. The mere art of it draws our attention—both men's and women's. Its simplicity, its complexity, its beauty draws us. Somewhere deep inside, below the level of most of our negatively influenced conscious thinking, it leaves us wondering why it's shaped the way it is.

I had to know why, and so I asked the Universe to show me, and It did. Not all at once, just a little bit at a time, and I probably don't have all the answers yet, but what I have I'll share, so follow me.

Looking at the shape of the head and tracing around the edge, following the curves and knowing the purpose that it serves—procreation and pleasure—it was telling me that the secrets of the Universe are held within its shape. Part of me questioned that revelation, but I knew it was true. I just *knew* it. In your mind, isolate that shape and trace around it, and let it speak to you. You'll see what I mean, the secrets of the Universe *are* within it.

Functionally, during intercourse, it acts like a round squeegee on the end of a plunger making sure the sexual fluids are forced deeply into the womb where conception can take place. With the in-stroke—thrust—the gentle rim pushes fluids inward, and on the out-stroke—withdrawal—it gathers the fluids along the back edge of the rim allowing them to be led by gravity down around to the bottom groove to be pushed in again by the next thrust. From an engineering standpoint, it is perfect. But then, again, nature always is.

But I knew there had to be more to its secrets. After all, sex isn't just for procreation. Simply put, it's about pleasure and love too. It's about coming together, and all that leads up to coming together—all the junk we go through, all the fears we overcome and, finally, the love that we feel when we are finally able to penetrate the barriers that have kept us apart. What does the penis have to say about that? What can we learn about sexuality or even about ourselves from its shape?

Let's start with a geometric shape called the cardioid shape. It appears throughout nature. It is basically a heart without a point. Leaves of many plants, such as a lily pad, are often that shape. The cross-section of the stems of many plants are also cardioid shaped. Some shell fish have that shape, and many other living organisms contain the cardioid shape somewhere within their structure. It is a basic shape in nature, and this fact seems to speak of its importance. I'm sure there is more significance to the shape than that and students of sacred geometry, I'm sure could add to it.

To generate a cardioid on paper is simple. Just trace one point on the edge of a circle as you rotate it around the perimeter of another circle of the same size. Another way is simply to cut a heart out of paper and trim off the point. Then, form it into a cone joining the two edges together where the curve is the sharpest, where the heart forms a groove. What you should have is a slightly flattened version of the head of a penis and, on a smaller scale, the clitoris. The most sensitive parts of our sexual organs are cardioid in shape. So simple yet containing so much mystery.

To further examine its mysteriousness, let us get theoretical for a few minutes. The following is oversimplified but only for the purpose of understanding it. In chaos theory, there is an equation that marks the point where chaos meets order, a point where chaos turns suddenly to order. It's like a theoretical membrane that separates chaos and order, and there is a particular mathematical equation that scientists have discovered that represents that point. Now, simple equations can easily be plotted on a graph so we can see the shape they represent. If you had high school algebra, you may remember plotting simple or even quadratic equations. We got straight lines or fancy curves, or whatever. In chaos theory, this equation, however, is quite complex and could not be plotted until we developed high-speed computers. When this equation was finally plotted, the shape that it generated was named a Mandelbrot Set. It belongs to a group of shapes called fractals, and they basically repeat themselves infinitely as the computer zooms in or zooms out.

The basic shape behind the Mandelbrot Set is the cardioid shape and as said earlier, it is basically a heart without a point. So, if you can imagine a cardioid, a heart without a point, around whose perimeter are connected other smaller cardioids and around them still smaller cardioids, basically, you have a Mandelbrot Set. Zooming in to any portion of its perimeter, you will see smaller cardioids upon even smaller cardioids upon smaller cardioids, etc.; zooming out, you will see the pattern repeated ad infinitum.

The remarkable thing about the Mandelbrot Set is that, theoretically, if you alter one small part of it, you are making that alteration to every part of it. It's holographic in that respect—the whole is contained in all of its parts. Change one part, and you've changed them all. What does this have to do with the penis and clitoris or, more generally, with sexuality?

The Divine Creator, Universe, or what ever you want to call the Creative Force, has chosen this shape for the organs through which we express our sexuality. This shape, that represents the point between chaos and order, is used to deliver our sexuality; thus, it represents the point of the ultimate coming together as human beings. When people overcome their fear of each other and of coming together and agree to have sex, then the point between fear and love is crossed—the same point that represents crossing from chaos to order. So, love becomes the ultimate order of the Universe.

The fact that this sacred shape has been chosen to deliver our sexuality indicates the sacredness and the significance of sexuality. Therefore our sexuality can be looked upon as our highest physical expression possible. Each sexual act, alone or with others, if consciously engaged in from a place of love, affects the whole Universe or, more correctly, taps into the Universal power of love. Realizing this, we can see that our sexuality is certainly not something over which to be embarrassed, shamed, guilty or judgmental. Rather, it is to shared, enjoyed even celebrated.

Think about that the next time you look at a penis— *and really look at it.*

Chapter 16

WHY CIRCUMCISION?
The Tip Off

CIRCUMCISION, a mutilating practice thousands of years old that actually removes sixty percent or more of the pleasure nerve endings of the penis, is now finally being questioned by many in the medical profession and is no longer covered by some insurance companies. In fact, information about reversal procedures is now widely available, especially on the Internet. Several years ago, I discovered a book entitled *The Joy of Uncircumcising* by Dr. Jim Bigelow. It describes a process of restoring to near-normal the foreskin of a circumcised male penis through a process of stretching the skin. I employed Dr. Bigelow's techniques, as well as some of my own innovations, with surprising results and benefits, including increased sensitivity. Unfortunately, lost nerve endings can never be replaced. This is not the main purpose of this article, however. The purpose is to examine possible origins and intent of circumcision.

Dr. Bigelow includes a good deal of information about

the surgical procedures used in the circumcision operation. What most of us think is a simple, painless procedure turns out not to be after all. *The operation has been performed on infants strapped to a board using no anesthetic.*

He also includes some historical information regarding the practice of circumcision, such as Yahweh's (Jehovah) ordering of circumcision as a symbol of his covenant with Abraham, as described in Genesis 17 of the *Old Testament* of the *Bible*. As far as most people who follow of one of the three Abrahamic religions, that is Judaism, Christianity and Islam, this reference tells us of the origin of the practice. He also mentions that the early Egyptians practiced circumcision prior to the time that Abraham lived. We know, too, from works such as Robert K. G. Temple's *The Sirius Mystery* that the Dogon tribe of northern Africa performed circumcision as part of their Sigui ceremony. This is a ceremony thousands of years old based on their phenomenal knowledge and connection with Sirius B (Digitaria), an invisible dwarf star that we didn't discover until the early 1900's. Circumcision remains a fundamental part of their religious rituals today. Thus, circumcision has perhaps affected more men throughout history than any other single religious or medical practice.

This leaves us with the burning questions of who started the practice and why. The "who," at least for now, remains an unanswered question. Perhaps it will always remain unanswered. As far as "why," we can at least speculate, and maybe that will shed some light on who. Let's first review the standard notions of why.

Rituals usually have some practical basis or origin. Could circumcision, used as a covenant between Yahweh and Abraham, serve as a mark of identification? Many religions today teach that it does. Was that the practical reason for the ritual? It does not seem logical, however, that circumcision was used for the purpose of identification considering the way it was originally performed. The early practice among the Jews was called Milah and removed only the tip of the foreskin, (frenar band) leaving practically the whole foreskin intact and hardly distinguishable from an uncircumcised male. There would better ways to achieve identification than a cut penis that looks almost like an uncut one, such as a tattoo or nipped earlobe (as was used to identify Israelite slaves). No, identification does not seem to be a logical explanation.

Other reasons that come to mind as to Why? are that it may have had to do with hygiene or to prevent masturbation. After reading Dr. Bigelow's book, it does not seem either of these reasons has much merit either.

Assuming for a moment that circumcision has religious roots, let's look at some religious ideas. As opposed to eastern religions as well as early and indigenous Pagan religions that teach sexuality can be a path to enlightenment, western religions teach that God stands up above, nature below, and man, with his animal sexual urges, struggles somewhere in between. In man's search for God, he must suppress his natural sexual urges. Therefore, controlling sex is necessary for man's own good. In this way sexual repression, which is limiting the ways sex can be experienced such as heterosexual monogamy only and forbidding masturbation, is seen as something desirable. Perhaps it was thought removal of sensitive, pleasure nerve endings would play a part in suppressing sexuality. It would hardly be as effective as imposing strict social and moral codes, which we know have successfully led to repressed sexuality. So, the argument for sexual repression is also weak and seems an unlikely reason for implementing circumcision.

The idea that circumcision was implemented as a means of control rather than identification still remains. There had to be a specific and practical reason for such a widespread practice. Whatever it is, like many ancient ritual practices, it continues today long after the original meaning has been forgotten.

After all the popular reasons given for the practice of circumcision are dismissed, we are left with the question Why? This is where we begin to speculate to connect some dots to see what we have.

Knowing that the basis for sky-god religions is that humans are slaves to a superior alien custodial race, that control is essential in maintaining the master/slave relationship and that circumcision had to have been of practical value, could it be that circumcision had to do with control? It is a good possibility so let's explore it.

If we homo-sapiens are, indeed, a slave race created through genetic engineering or, more specifically, through unplugging and deactivating strands of DNA, the engineering would have included attempts by the custodians to remove any and all memory or our previous existence. Any memory of who or what we were originally as spiritual beings would have to be removed in order to prevent us from awakening and ultimately rebelling. These attempts would have included shutting down or removing any parts or systems of the human body or psyche that possibly contained any cosmic memory. Let's explore the concept and possibility of such a memory or cosmic memory existing.

Reflexologists believe that the feet, hands and even ear lobes contain nerve endings that correspond to other parts of the body. When these points are stimulated, healing of the corresponding organ can occur. In a similar belief within in the practice of Tantra sex, the penis and clitoris contain nerve endings that correspond to other body parts as well. It is believed that the very tip of the penis and the clitoris correspond to the top of the head, the area of the crown chakra—the seat of our spirituality.

It is also recognized by any good body worker or massage therapist that our body's muscular structures contain memories of events from our past or from our

127

childhood. Putting these two bits of information together, could the penis and clitoris, which contain nerve endings that correspond to the crown chakra, contain cosmic memories?

Could the body itself or even individual cells contain cosmic memories of our origin in a similar manner that a broken piece of a hologram picture contains the picture of the whole? More specifically, could the penis and the clitoris, the primary organs involved in pleasure and reproduction, contain a memory of our cosmic origins or past? Thus, could the ordering of circumcision (removal of part of the foreskin) and excision (removal of the clitoris) be desperate but futile attempts by Yahweh or other sky-gods to remove any remaining cosmic memory—memories which might help us to awaken to our cosmic reality, our spirituality? In addition, could this explain the extreme, deep-felt anger and resentment some men in our society have toward being circumcised as expressed in Dr. Bigelow's book? These possibilities deserve our attention.

If the answers to these questions is "Yes," it would be consistent with the theories of William Bramley in *The Gods of Eden*, Zecharia Sitchin in his *Earth Chronicles* series, as well as Dr. Arthur David Horn in *Humanity's Extraterrestrial Origins*. These three distinguished researchers seem to think there is sufficient evidence to believe that we have been, and possibly still are, slaves to a more technically advanced group or groups of beings. If so,

128

what I have just outlined regarding the origins of circumcision is a possibility.

But, let's not stop here. Taking this one step further, it is also a possibility then, that by continuing this 'religious' procedure we may, indeed, be impeding our own spiritual growth, and by discontinuing circumcision (both male and female) we could actually hasten our spiritual enlightenment and independence from these "sky gods." However, regardless if any of this is true, let us free ourselves of this painful, mutilating procedure since there is no practical justification of it for us today.

Chapter 17

MEDIBATION

MEDIBATION OR *MEDIBATING*, as the term implies, combines the practice of meditation and masturbation. I first heard of the term through the work of Annie Sprinkle, famous sex film star and sex educator. She refers to her own spiritual work and practice of *medibation* in some of her written work as well as in her film, *Masturbation Memoirs* and her video, *Herstory of Porn*. While I discovered the name *medibation* a couple of years ago, I had discovered the process several years earlier, and so when I first read and saw Annie's work, I knew precisely what she was talking about.

I had discover this practice quite by accident. While masturbation had been part of my life since a teenager, I had never taken it beyond the "it just feels good" sex-play stages. Likewise, I had practiced meditation for probably a good ten years, and it had led me to many peaceful moments as well as many insights. Until then, the two experiences had been quite separate—or so I thought. What was probably happening was that a process was unfolding whereby the two would necessarily come together.

The two practices, masturbation and meditation, came together in my conscious mind while I was writing an article about my experience with an obscure Dr. Seuss book called *The Seven Lady Godivas.* I had been working slowly on the piece, writing, rewriting, etc. for a couple of weeks. During this time. I began my days, as usual, with the same morning ritual I had practiced for a number of years. I would wake up early, have a cup of coffee and slowly masturbate to orgasm, then go back to sleep to enjoy those ensuing twenty minutes or so of totally relaxing post-orgasmic bliss before getting up and starting my day. During the time I was working on this piece of writing, however, my mind would not just randomly drift off during my post-orgasm high as it usually had done, but I would find myself thinking about what I had written the previous day.

But it was *more* than just thinking about it. I would actually see the typed pages it in front of me as I dozed. The pages would scroll down past my field of vision, and I could see the printed words on the pages. Occasionally the scrolling would stop, and the page would zoom in so I could get a closer look. Whenever that occurred, there was always something there that needed to be changed or rewritten. Once I made a mental note of the needed correction, the scrolling would resume.

This process would not occupy the entire twenty

minute session of post orgasmic bliss,just a portion of it. The rest of the time I would find myself either reliving my *Seven Lady Godiva* experience and composing the next section to be written, or I would be thinking about and gaining insights and direction into some other matter that I needed to attend to that day.

During the time of writing this piece, I consciously became aware of this process and began to look forward to it each morning. I finished the piece in about three weeks and it remains one that I am proud of. I continue to use this process now, and it has led me to incredible insights—all the while bringing a lot of pleasure too.

My practice of medibation today, however, goes farther now than it did in the earlier days. Today it includes far more than daily problem solving. It brings me many insights into my purpose for being on this planet as well as a sense of Oneness to everything. And,one of the most important parts of it is prayer. I find that it is the best time to pray because the very nature of having an orgasm requires total surrender. It is in that mind-set, then, that we can offer our prayers—most of all, prayers of gratitude—beginning with gratitude for sex itself, and then, for all of life. Perhaps that is the greatest insight that has come to me through medibation—GRATITUDE.

* * *

What other authors say:

"NAKED BEFORE GOD: A Look at Healing, Self-discovery and Spiritual Growth through Social Nudism combines insight, great humor and fascinating anecdotes to tell the account of Mr. Ziegler's personal quest for self-discovery. Discarding clothing, both a symbol *of* and fortress *for* anti-sexual, anti-natural uptightness, Daniel Ziegler has proven that the most basic path to the soul is acceptance and love for the body."
–Daniel Blair Stewart, author of *TESLA: The Modern Sorcerer* and *AKHUNATON: The Extraterrestrial King.*

"I met Dan Ziegler and was immediately attached to his intelligence. He was, to me, an enlightened soul. But a huge red light came on when I learned he was a practicing nudist; the subject of social nudism was a matter of embarrassed laughter for my friends and myself. I vowed to not see or talk with Dan ever again. However, he had given me his manuscript *NAKED BEFORE GOD: A Look at Healing, Self-discovery and Spiritual Growth through Social Nudism*. The red light aspect drew me to his words, but the shear clarity it evoked about self-acceptance gave me the courage to visit a nudist park in a green light mode. I've never looked back."
–Shirley Swift, author of Michigan historical fiction: *LEGACY OF FIVE WIVES REMEMBERED* and *DEADLY GAME.*